Medieval Lyric

For *Charlotte* and *Mossman Roueché*

Edited with
an Introduction
and Commentary
by

John C. Hirsh

Medieval Lyric

Middle
English
Lyrics,
Ballads,
and
Carols

b **Blackwell**
Publishing

Editorial material and organization © 2005 by Blackwell Publishing Ltd

BLACKWELL PUBLISHING
350 Main Street, Malden, MA 02148-5020, USA
108 Cowley Road, Oxford OX4 1JF, UK
550 Swanston Street, Carlton, Victoria 3053, Australia

First published 2005 by Blackwell Publishing Ltd

Library of Congress Cataloging-in-Publication Data

Medieval lyric : Middle English lyrics, ballads, and carols / edited
with an introduction and commentary / by John C. Hirsh.
    p. cm.
Includes bibliographical references and indexes.
ISBN 1–4051–1481–9 (alk. paper) — ISBN 1–4051–1482–7 (pbk. : alk.
paper)
    1. English poetry—Middle English, 1100–1500.   2. English
poetry—Middle English, 1100–1500—Modernized versions.   3. Ballads,
English—England—Texts.   4. Carols, English—England—Texts.   I. Hirsh,
John C.

PR1120.M375 2005
821′.040801—dc22

                                                          2003026892

A catalogue record for this title is available from the British Library.

Set in 10/12.5pt Dante
by Graphicraft Ltd, Hong Kong
Printed and bound in the United Kingdom
by MPG Books Ltd, Bodmin, Cornwall

The publisher's policy is to use permanent paper from mills that operate a
sustainable forestry policy, and which has been manufactured from pulp
processed using acid-free and elementary chlorine-free practices. Furthermore,
the publisher ensures that the text paper and cover board used have met
acceptable environmental accreditation standards.

For further information on
Blackwell Publishing, visit our website:
http://www.blackwellpublishing.com

Contents

Illustrations

Preface

For about a decade, roughly between 1965 and 1975, the publication and critical examination of medieval lyrical poetry was one of the hottest areas in the study of English medieval literature, both in Britain and in America. Rosemary Woolf's widely anticipated 1968 study *The English Religious Lyric in the Middle Ages* appeared in the same year as the revised edition of Peter Dronke's *Medieval Latin and the Rise of European Love-Lyric*. Taken together the two works, one carefully developing the traditions within which the English lyric expressed itself, the other concerned with the extent to which the medieval lyric poet, writing in Latin, was in dialogue with those traditions so as to express his individuality and originality, seemed to generate interest in a genre which had not heretofore been regarded as central to what was then confidently regarded as the medieval literary canon. In the next year Sarah Appleton Weber's *Theology and Poetry in the Middle English Lyric*, and in 1972 two studies, Douglas Gray's *Themes and Images in the Medieval English Religious Lyric*, and Edmund Reiss' *The Art of the Middle English Lyric*, though proceeding from very different critical assumptions, provided a new view of the medieval English lyric, one which emphasized poetic individuality and aesthetic novelty, and which revealed an attachment and contribution to a European poetic tradition and convention which had not been much noted before. Both the decade itself and the energy which had offered so many new readings of English lyrical texts seemed to give way to other, sometimes theoretical concerns after the publication of Gray's *Selection of Religious Lyrics*, which appeared in the Clarendon Medieval and Tudor Series in 1975.

In the intervening thirty years other studies have appeared, and, no doubt at least in part because of the work I have just described, the lyric is no longer as marginalized as it once was, though it is certainly possible to believe that the emphasis on individual poetic accomplishment present in most of the studies I have just cited had the effect of limiting its appeal to those whose theories, from the late 1970s on, led elsewhere. Recently, though, it has become possible again to speak without apology both of literature and of individual poetic practice, a circumstance which has led to a kind of lyrical *renovatio*, in which studies in gender and culture, among others, have led to a reauthorization of these extraordinary texts, having discovered in them modes and means of expression not elsewhere available, and also a richness of implication and nuance which had appealed as well to the earlier investigators. This new interest has, in recent years, reached out to the study of carols and ballads, as the question of their medieval roots, uses, and practices is raised again, and the traditional literary-historical formulations are called into question. This edition is a contribution to these new concerns and these new readings, and, while not at all ignoring earlier readings and contributions, seeks to engage students in the serious study of the extraordinarily interesting texts printed here.

In the course of my work I have incurred many debts, not all of them financial. I am most grateful to the libraries which preserve the manuscripts upon which this edition is based for permission to work in their collections, and to publish edited versions of texts based upon their holdings, and I am equally grateful to the librarians who assisted me in my labors. These include: Balliol College Library, Oxford; the Bodleian Library, Oxford; the British Library, London; Cambridge University Library; the Eton College Library, Windsor; Gonville and Caius College Library, Cambridge; Lambeth Palace Library, London; Trinity College Library, Cambridge; and Worcester Cathedral Library. I am also grateful to the Archive of Folk Culture and to the American Folklife Center of the Library of Congress for assistance with my study of the ballad. More personally, my greatest debt is to Douglas Gray, J. R. R. Tolkien Professor of English Literature Emeritus at Oxford, not only for generously reading and commenting upon my manuscript, but, more than 30 years earlier, for introducing me both to the study of the medieval English lyric itself, and to those who were speeding its examination, in particular Peter Dronke, Professor of Latin Literature Emeritus at Cambridge, who kindly gave permission to print his translation of "Foebus abierat" in the introduction to part IX, and the late pioneering scholars Rossell Hope Robbins and Rosemary Woolf. The sense of innovation and discovery which attended upon those early days resides still in the lyrics themselves, and in the work which these scholars produced, and seems to me available as well to any who actively engage them.

Other debts are less direct but not less real. I am particularly grateful to Thomas Niles of New York and to John Edward Niles of Silver Spring, Maryland, who together hold the copyright of *The Ballad Book of John Jacob Niles*, for permission to publish the American versions of five ballads which appear in part IX below, and which their father, the great American student of ballads John Jacob Niles, collected in Appalachia during the 1930s. The copyright for these ballads, as for the *Ballad Book* itself, remains with them. I am also most grateful to Eudora

Richardson of Georgetown for having introduced me to Thomas Niles, some years since. At Georgetown I have profited from the work and advice of Sarah McNamer, herself a distinguished student of the Middle English lyric, and also from the general counsel and good example of my closest colleagues in medieval literature at Georgetown, Jo Ann H. Moran Cruz, Penn R. Szittya, and Kelley M. Wickham-Crowley. At Georgetown too I have benefitted from the often perceptive comments of students in many different courses, and it was the evident interest of these students in lyrics and ballads in particular that encouraged me to proceed with this edition. In Oxford my work has been assisted, in ways too many and various to record, by Helen Cooper, P. Jeremy Fairhead, Neil Ferguson, OP, Rev. Dr Harriet Harris, Laura C. H. Hoyano, Jörn Leonhard, and Bernard O'Donoghue. In London my greatest personal debts are to my friends Charlotte and Mossman Roueché, to whom I have dedicated the volume.

This edition was begun in 2000 when I was a Keeley Visiting Fellow at Wadham College, Oxford, and I warmly record my gratitude to the then-Warden, the late John Flemming, and to all the fellowship, for my election and support. At Georgetown I am also grateful to David W. Lightfoot, Dean of the Graduate School, for supplying a grant-in-aide, which helped. I am further grateful to Andrew McNeillie, former Literature Editor at Blackwells, and to Emma Bennett and Karen Wilson, also of Blackwells, for their help and support with this project. I am most grateful as well to Anna Oxbury, whose evident knowledge and interest was of real help in the editorial process.

Georgetown University,
Washington, D.C.

Abbreviations

The following works are cited throughout, the earlier editions at the beginning of each poem:

Allen: Hope Emily Allen, ed., *English Writings of Richard Rolle, Hermit of Hampole* (Oxford: Clarendon Press, 1931).

Ballad Book: *The Ballad Book of John Jacob Niles* (Boston: Houghton Mifflin, 1961, rpt. New York: Dover Publications, 1970).

Brown A: Carleton Brown, ed., *English Lyrics of the XIIIth Century* (Oxford: Clarendon Press, 1932, rpt, 1965).

Brown B: Carleton Brown, ed., *Religious Lyrics of the XIVth Century*, second edition, revised by G. V. Smithers (Oxford: Clarendon Press, 1957).

Brown C: Carleton Brown, ed., *Religious Lyrics of the XVth Century* (Oxford: Clarendon Press, 1939, rpt. 1962).

Brown Collection: *The Frank G. Brown Collection of North Carolina Folklore*, Newman Ivey White, general editor, 7 volumes (Durham, N.C.: Duke University Press, 1952–64). The ballads are cited from volume 2: *Folk Ballads from North Carolina*, Henry M. Belden and Arthur Palmer Hudson, eds. (1952). Music for the ballads is printed in volume 4 (1957).

Child: Francis James Child, ed., *The English and Scottish Popular Ballads*, 5 volumes (Boston and New York: Houghton, Mifflin; London: Henry Stevens Sons and Stiles, 1882–1898, rpt. New York: Dover Publications, 1965).

Coffin: Tristram Potter Coffin, *The British Traditional Ballad in North America*. Revised edition with a supplement by Robert deV. Renwick. Bibliographical and Special Series, The American Folklore Society (Austin and London: University of Texas Press, 1977).

Davies: R. T. Davies, ed., *Middle English Lyrics: A Critical Anthology* (London: Faber and Faber; Chicago: Northwestern University Press, 1964).

Duncan A: Thomas G. Duncan, ed., *Medieval English Lyrics, 1200–1400*, Penguin Classics (Harmondsworth: Penguin Books, 1995).

Duncan B: Thomas G. Duncan, ed., *Late Medieval English Lyrics and Carols, 1400–1530*, Penguin Classics (Harmondsworth: Penguin Books, 2000).

Gray: Douglas Gray, ed., *A Selection of Religious Lyrics*, Clarendon Medieval and Tudor Series (Oxford: Clarendon Press, 1975; rpt. Exeter, 1992).

Greene: Richard L. Greene, ed., *The Early English Carols*, second edition (Oxford: Clarendon Press, 1977).

IMEV: *The Index of Middle English Verse*, Carleton Brown and Rossell Hope Robbins, eds. (New York: Columbia University Press for The Index Society, 1943).

Randolph: *Ozark Folksongs*, Vance Randolph, ed., 4 volumes, revised edition (Columbia, Mo. and London: University of Missouri Press, 1980). The ballads are cited from volume 1: *British Ballads and Songs* (1980).

Reimer: Stephen R. Reimer, ed., *The Works of William Herebert, OFM*, Studies and Texts 81 (Toronto: Pontifical Institute of Medieval Studies, 1987).

Robbins: Rossell Hope Robbins, ed., *Secular Lyrics of the XIVth and XVth Centuries*, second edition (Oxford: Clarendon Press, 1955).

SC: Falconer Madden, et al., *A Summary Catalogue of Western Manuscripts in the Bodleian Library at Oxford*, 7 volumes in 8 (Oxford: Clarendon Press, 1895–1953).

Supplement: *Supplement to the Index of Middle English Verse*, Rossell Hope Robbins and Jonathan L. Cutler, eds. (Lexington: University of Kentucky Press, 1965).

Whiting: Ella Keats Whiting, ed., *The Poems of John Audelay*, OS 184 (London: Oxford University Press for the Early English Text Society, 1931).

Introduction

This is an anthology of medieval poetry both interesting and excellent, for which I have made the reader's imaginative understanding of the text and context my first consideration in selecting, editing, and commenting upon each of the poems which follow, while keeping in mind the critical and philological requirements of a student of medieval texts. Remembering that "Best sentence and moost solaas" was Chaucer's standard for the tales his pilgrims were to tell, I have chosen poems which open to the reader important aspects of their art, religion, and culture, and which can be read with interest by students either beginning or continuing their examination of medieval literature. These poems offer an insight into the workings of medieval poetic practice, if only because the best English lyrics, ballads, and carols, are as good as any written or composed in Europe during the period, and when their attention to diction, word-play, idealized and empirical images are taken into account, they can be understood to have informed modern poetic practice, too. But they offer as well an insight into the workings of medieval culture itself, both in its religious practices and in its secular constructions.

Directions and Beginnings

Medieval Christianity, at once lyrical and severe, powerfully attuned to the responsiveness of the individual Christian and also to teachings concerning Christ, his mother, the Church, and the saints, is fully represented here, as are the joy and apprehension, the freedom and doubt, the celebration and the reflectiveness which attended upon medieval Christian life. In a way difficult to describe but less difficult to understand, the medieval religious lyric, particularly in the vernacular, speaks directly of those values, attitudes, and assumptions which made up the religious life of the articulate, faithful, and devout individual Christian. It is usual, especially in the study of pre-Reformation British religiousness, to turn to the ubiquitous handbooks of spiritual guidance, written usually by men and as often by clerics, in order to discern and define the states – or more often the stages – of spiritual development, and the kinds of mental engagement practiced. But religious lyrics equally, and often with greater responsiveness, reveal and even define those attitudes. We sometimes find in these lyrics the studied, even pedagogical introduction to the practice of devotion present in the devotional handbooks. But more often what emerges is the result of that engagement, one which sometimes reveals or encodes the birth or the growth of religious attitudes. That development is often less reasoned than those which the handbooks taught, and usually is closer in tone to what the fourteenth-century English mystic Richard Rolle recorded of his revelations, which came to him "suddenly and unknown." This same sense of *dis*connection is present too in the leaps of mind and of spirit which certain of the lyrics record, and in the sense of wonder many reveal. In their own way then, the best of the vernacular religious lyrics bring us as close to an understanding of the actual practice, celebration, and experience of medieval religiousness as any other source, though given their poetic origins, the understanding which they hold out is always in some sense conditional.

But all was not religion. Medieval secular life flourishes among these lyrics too, at once witty and bawdy, celebratory and ironic, bitter and joyous. For all of their apparently universal appeal, many of these secular lyrics originated in, or at least were associated with, courtly and noble audiences, as were many of the manuscripts which still preserve them. Secular lyrics sometimes echo, in homage or in irony, religious ones, though they carve out their own way too, and the tradition of secular lyric poetry and secular songs written in English, which is now so universal, begins in the late medieval period. For reasons of culture and audience, secular lyrics lent themselves to parody and satire more easily than religious lyrics did, though in the hands of a master, like Geoffrey Chaucer, the parody could take on a life of its own, enriching the language and the poetic tradition both. It was in this period, after all, that secular lyric poetry made its appearance in English, preparing the way for the rich and powerful mixture of love, politics, sorrow, celebration, angst, irony, joy, and detachment which register so powerfully in lyrics, songs, and poems today.

I have divided this anthology into ten parts, and purposefully, I have not put all themes or like poems together. Thus, carols can be found elsewhere than in their assigned section, religious themes erupt in the midst of love poetry, and allusions to sex register throughout. It is important to remember how very diverse and also how varied Middle English lyrics are, whether secular or religious, and also how widespread they and their influence proved to be. Attitudes toward the uses of learning (many of the authors were clerics, both young and old), toward the meaning of Christian life, toward the practice of poetry, toward love and toward sex, change from poet to poet, from lyric to lyric. It is true that certain of the poems echo – and occasionally resist – each other, but it is equally true that in doing so they identify and define values, attitudes, and assumptions which at once spring from and inform the poetic practices in which their makers engaged.

The Medieval Lyric

There are quite literally thousands of lyrics preserved in English from the medieval period, and although their connection to Old English poems is still a matter of discussion and even dispute,[1] the genre as a whole appears to have taken on a new life, if not actually sprung into being, in the thirteenth century, rather later than elsewhere in Europe, but at a time when the friars, new religious orders like the Franciscans, followers of St. Francis of Assisi (1182–1226), and Dominicans, followers of St. Dominic (1172–1221), dedicated themselves not to living in isolation in monasteries (Christian monasticism first appeared in Egypt and Palestine late in the third century, though its most important growth took place under the influence of St. Benedict of Nursia (d. 550)), but rather to preaching the word of God to the people, whom they thus sought to lead to salvation. Many lyrics were undoubtedly written for this commendable purpose, though friars wrote lyrics as well for each other and simply for the joy of making poetry, while others who were not friars also took up the practice, inscribing, singing, and reciting poems, both secular and religious, many of which, thankfully, found their way into medieval manuscripts, and have so come down to us.[2]

The initial explosion of Middle English lyric poetry was thus like a Russian spring, yet like a real Russian spring, it was the product of deep roots, which were founded in Old English linguistic and even poetic traditions, in Latin literature and Christian liturgy, in vernacular music, song, and dance, in theological nuance and doctrine, and in philosophical teaching and distinction. Its origins reached back to the beginnings of Christianity itself, when songs were sung in imitation of the hymns inscribed by Homer, Pindar, and many others in honor of the Greek and Roman gods. Early accounts of devout Christian practices, in particular one contained in a letter Pliny the Younger (c.61–112) addressed to the emperor Trajan concerning his examination of some Christians whom he had in custody, records those Christians singing in the pre-dawn hours (*ante lucem*) songs or hymns "to Christ as to a god" (*Christo quasi deo*) (*Ep.* 10.96). Hilarius of Poitiers (d. 368), drawing upon Byzantine tradition, composed, perhaps for the first time in the West, a *Liber Hymnorum*, to be used in services by the congregation. Wherever begun, this practice was taken up and advanced by, among others, Ambrose of Milan (d. 397), who, as Chadwick remarks, popularized the congregational hymn "in order to identify with the values of the *plebs*," since singing involved both genders, and the rich and the poor alike.[3]

The moral and psychological support which the congregational singing of hymns provides proved particularly helpful during a period of difficulty with the authorities, and it is possible that the practice took root, or at least developed apace, around about the time of the Arian persecution in 386. In any event, a celebrated follower of Ambrose, Augustine of Hippo (354–430) specifically records in his *Confessions* (IX 7.15) that it was during such a time that "the decision was taken to introduce hymns and psalms [*hymni et psalmi*] sung after the custom of the eastern Churches [*secundum morem orientalium*], to prevent the people from succumbing to depression and exhaustion. From that time to this day the practice has been retained and many, indeed almost all your flocks, in other parts of the world [*et per cetera orbis*] have imitated it."[4] The roots of the religious lyric were in song, and the roots of religious song may have been there.

The Byzantine musical tradition which came eventually to feed the West was itself the product of deliberate ecclesiastical policy and studied artistic innovation. "The great basilica churches of the eastern world had become places of newly elaborated liturgical drama," Peter Brown writes. "They offered a form of 'sacred theater' which strove to rival the ever-present 'Church of Satan' – the ancient theater and the Hippodrome. The hymns of Romanos Melodes, a Syrian immigrant to Constantinople who wrote in the days of Justinian, filled the churches with a new, high form of religious poetry. Borrowed from Syria, the chanted hymn, the *kontakion*, was a religious form as novel and as stunning, in its own way, as the Baroque *oratorio*."[5] These deep liturgical resonances fed a related sense of wonder and reverence which remains, changes having been made, in certain medieval religious lyrics, though secular lyrics from the same period sometimes oppose them explicitly. Still, their usual effect was to add a religious and musical resonance to the poems they informed, and to lend an air of orthodoxy to their tone – even when the poem itself was not specifically (or not at all) concerned to be orthodox.

It is good to remember that, sudden as the appearance of vernacular lyrics in thirteenth-century Britain may have been, they were already well established on the continent. In southern France the sophisticated, witty, and sharp songs of the troubadours begin in the eleventh century, and those of Guillaume IX (1071–1127) the seventh Count of Poitiers and the ninth Duke of Aquitaine, among the earliest which have come down to us, are so deeply invested in the persona of the poet, that unlike many of the English lyrics, it is hardly possible to ignore it. But certain other troubadour practices are not entirely dissimilar to what appeared in England. Thus Bernart de Ventadorn's great lyric "Car vei la lauzeta mover" ("When I see the lark moving") begins with the opening of the *Kyrie eleison* of the *Cum jubilo* mass.[6] The easy linking of sacred song and secular convention

hardly began in England, though the forms which the practice took were sometimes more orthodox there, and often were resolved in favor of the sacred, not
the other way.[7]

But precedence did not belong only to France. In Germany the Minnesang
sprang to life in the twelfth century, and by the time Dante Alighieri (1265–
1321) came to write his brilliant lyrics, there was already present in Italy a
century-old tradition of vernacular lyric poetry waiting for him to adapt and
transform. Indeed, the thirst for vernacular lyric poetry was so great in Italy that
the poems themselves appear in the most unlikely of places. Among the official
registers of contracts and wills in Bologna in the late thirteenth and early fourteenth
century at least one notary would fill in the blank spaces at the end of his official
entries with songs which he either knew by heart or had recently heard sung in
the street.[8] These additions had a practical intention – they sought to prevent
forgeries in the registers by the insertions of new entries in the otherwise blank
spaces – but some of the songs thus recorded are not known from any other
source, and so remind us of the extraordinary popularity which vernacular lyric
poetry enjoyed throughout Europe, and how many lyrics, in all probability, we
have lost. This European vernacular tradition, following hard upon the heels of
the medieval Latin one, can encourage the student to ask serious questions of
the English lyrics which follow, since many of the questions they pose concerning
point of view, voice, intention, and the role of the poet, are intrinsic to the genre.[9]

The Middle English Lyric

Following the Norman invasion of 1066, English, as a literary language, became
all but submerged in Latin and in Anglo-Norman, so that texts which previously
would have been written in, or translated into, the spoken language of the English
people became fewer in number – though it is important to remember that they
never entirely disappeared. It is therefore both surprising and pleasing that
Middle English lyrics, both secular and (especially) sacred, appear suddenly and
in really extraordinary numbers in the manuscript record relatively early in the
thirteenth century, and continue almost without interruption well into the sixteenth. The manuscripts cited in this edition suggest that during this period the
audience expanded considerably, becoming decidedly more secularized, though
never losing its religious base, both among the clergy and increasingly among
the laity. The religious poems are informed throughout by traditions of devotion and prayer which are identifiably British, though these traditions, rooted
in pre-conquest spirituality, were themselves modified under continental influence, and the poems in turn reflect these alterations as the centuries proceed,
so that the religious poems in particular come to represent, often starkly, both

Christ's suffering at the time of his Passion and the almost requisite responsiveness of the individual Christian. There seems very little doubt that the entrance into England of the orders of friars, particularly the Franciscans, had a real effect upon the production of lyrical poetry, by providing religious, vocational, and ideological justification for the writing of religious poems, and by inculcating the sense that such poems could make both religious faith and the teachings of the Church attractive to the ordinary Christian.[10]

But it is clear too that, over the centuries, they came to draw on a large number of other sources, passages from Latin sermons and popular devotional texts like the Prymer among them.[11] Although it is very difficult to say with confidence exactly when many lyrics were written, there was both change and development in the Middle English lyric at several stages, and in particular from the middle of the thirteenth century onwards, not only by the addition of new themes, narrative variation, and continental influences, but also in the latitude which poets permitted themselves in developing authorial voice and address, and indeed in almost all forms of poetic expression. Throughout this period, many Middle English lyrics were indebted, directly or not, to literary developments begun in narrative art forms, whether in their narrative tone, the voice of their persona, or even in their development of symbolic notation. These influences could overlap and interact with existing practices, so that it is difficult, on the basis of internal evidence alone, to fix the priority of these developments with any confidence, or to say definitively that this change grew out of that practice.[12]

Although I have focused in this anthology on the great wealth of anonymous lyrics preserved from the late medieval period, I have included in the first two appendices examples of lyrics by known English authors: Geoffrey Chaucer, then as now universally recognized as the greatest of medieval English poets; William Herebert, OFM (d. c.1333), a learned Franciscan academic and preacher who was Lector in Theology at the Franciscan house in Oxford, 1317–19; Richard Rolle (d. 1349), a very well-known mystic from Yorkshire; and John Audelay, a blind Augustinian cleric and chaplain of the fifteenth century, all of whom adapted the lyric's traditional conventions when they themselves wrote new ones. Chaucer's own lyrics are all but *sui generis*, and repeatedly press at the boundaries of the very form of the lyric itself. The effective and affecting English lyrics of the sophisticated English Franciscan William Herebert, who was also the author of a number of polished Latin sermons, provide examples of the sort of formal, even conventional, but felt texts which a dedicated Franciscan preacher could produce. Though perhaps lacking the sophistication of his Latin sermons, the poems engage their audience by their attention to clear, even hard, diction and detail, and by their studied orthodoxy.

No less dedicated to his vocation and his art was the blind poet John Audelay, who may have been somewhat less intellectual than other such authors, but who drew upon a depth of religious feeling which showed his familiarity with the English devotional tradition, even though he was capable of sounding secular themes within the same poem. Earlier, the mystic Richard Rolle had written lyrics which were equally religious, and not at all constrained by liturgical practice. Rolle's lyrics reveal the love-longing that the poet himself experienced for the divine, and reflect the holy love and "gastly gladness" (spiritual joy) which were integral to his mysticism. His lyrics though, like Herebert's, included a homiletic effect, which was as intended as the poetic. Indeed many poets in this period (possibly not Chaucer, however) would have regarded the distinction as meaningless, since the poems were finally constructed and concerned to praise and reveal the ultimate reality which was God.[13]

Relatively early, religious poems began to interact with secular ones, really to the advantage of both, so that in the later periods it is no longer possible to tell at the beginning of an English poem whether it will proceed to a sacred or a secular resolution. One other circumstance which informs English lyrics, and which they share with their continental counterparts, is the extent to which women, sometimes apparently excluded from medieval authorship, wrote them. It is interesting to speculate too that lyric poetry may have offered one of the first opportunities for women to articulate emotions like love and resentment, devotion and impatience, which is present in the Western literary canon. In her examination of lyric poems preserved in the Findern manuscript, four of whose poems I have printed here, including three in Appendix C, Sarah McNamer has pointed out that not only were many of the poems which the manuscript contains written by women, but that they are among the first "self-expressive" examples of lyric poetry in English, and constitute an "authentic woman's lament"; further evidence for the circumstances of women's authorship is now emerging in examinations of the books that they owned and read.[14] One other factor which aided in women's authorship, however, and which has not yet been thoroughly explored, concerns the extent to which secular lyrics were written at court, and so enjoyed both courtly and noble associations; in both of these women figured importantly.

Certainly some of the manuscripts which contain the best secular lyrics were produced at court or were associated with it, and particularly from the time of King Richard II (1367–1400, reigned 1377–99), English poetry was widely read and written in the fourteenth-century English court, as many lyrics (and their manuscripts) testify.[15] Past commentary did not emphasize courtly associations even of individual lyrics, perhaps partly because some of the very best collections of Middle English lyrics had their origins elsewhere. British Library manuscript, MS Sloane 2593, for example, now only a fragment of what was once a much longer early fifteenth-century manuscript, contains one of the very best collections of sacred and secular Middle English lyrics, but is clearly associated with Bury St Edmunds, almost certainly with the great Benedictine abbey there. Likewise, the quite extraordinary collection made in the first third of the sixteenth century and now preserved at Balliol College, Oxford, as MS 354, which describes itself as "A Boke of dyueris tales and balettes [ballads] and dyueris Reconynges etc.," was largely written by one Richard Hill, a prominent London grocer and merchant, though evidently one with an eye for good poetry and song, among other (more unusual) texts.[16]

Still, even though some manuscripts containing secular lyrics do have undeniably courtly associations, there seems not to have been the tradition in England, as there was in France, of the nobility causing lavish manuscripts to be written which preserved illustrated and decorated lyrical poems.[17] But it was certainly the court's influence that precipitated, perhaps even caused, the developed sense of an English nation, brilliantly reflected in carols like "The Agincourt Carol" (no. 49). Even without the courtly associations present in other lyrics, this carol achieves, in its repeated *Deo gracias*, a sense of the divine protection which King Henry V (1386–1422, reigned 1413–22) claimed for his 1415 victory, and which is present in so many Middle English lyrics and carols, but which is here attached to the actions of the state. Throughout the canon of Middle English lyric poetry, however, whether written by men or by women, clerics or courtiers, English lyrics display an empirical tendency, a somewhat limited employment of literary convention for its own sake, and, in many cases, a kind of tough liveliness which sets them apart from many of their European cousins, as their attention to diction and to public attitude lends them both power and interest.

Ballads, Carols, and One Other Point

This freshness, often accompanied by a sense of wonder, carries forward from the Middle English lyric into the (somewhat later) ballads and carols, which can be documented only from the late thirteenth century, so that any connection with songs sung in earlier periods, whether in Britain or elsewhere, must be largely conjectural. When exactly true folk ballads began is still in doubt, though it is possible to believe that, whatever their origin may have been (I have printed Peter Dronke's translation of an early poem informed by balladic practice, along with an extended introduction to recent critical attitudes toward the study of ballads, as an introduction to Part IX, below), the genre itself took root in the period after the twelfth century when evidence for medieval song becomes more widely available. Still, it has in the past been argued that ballads developed relatively late in the medieval period, and were informed, in many cases deeply, by the circumstances of their recitation and oral transmission. In

England, Robin Hood ballads became particularly widespread in the fifteenth century, and were among the earliest to gain a general audience. Whether a person named "Robin Hood" actually existed or not, and the leading Robin Hood scholar today, Stephen Knight, has convincingly argued that he did not, the songs and ballads as a group attest to an interest in vernacular narrative and ballads so developed that it is difficult to believe that it only began late in the preceding century.[18] The studied *naïveté* of many late ballads, together with the often quite spurious historical information which they contain, suggest the presence, persistence, and importance of minstrel-redactors in transmitting and even formulating the ballad, and not that the ballads sprang either from now lost "folk origins" or from the emending pens of Tudor or Stewart antiquaries.

The closer we look at balladic variation the more apparent the hand (and the voice) of the individual performer or redactor becomes. Repeatedly revised and added to, cut and redefined, ballads are rarely fixed (except when one version or another appears in print), and, as persons and populations shift, so ballads move with them. Many of the greatest medieval ballads appear again in twentieth-century America, sung by folk singers who were unaware of their medieval roots, while others were adapted from songs anonymously encountered. Often these later products, like their medieval ancestors, utilize a kind of conscious archaizing in which simple motivation, dramatic incident, and powerful (if suppressed) emotion emerge clearly in performance.[19]

Changes having been made, the same issues, though not the same solutions, inform the origin and composition of carols, though the fact that these are better attested than ballads throughout the late medieval period, together with the universal presence of a refrain (or "burden") as a defining characteristic, indicate a frequent degree of communal participation, often sprung from dance, in their origin and performance. The contemporary identification of carols with the celebration of Christmas has obscured their medieval variety and popularity, when they could celebrate everything from a military victory to Mary's virginity. But it is not difficult to see in them the mixture of poetic convention and felt purpose, warning and celebration, art and artlessness, which equally can be found in the medieval English lyric.[20]

One final point. Reading poetry is never a static process. Certain of the poems which follow – whether lyrics, ballads, or carols – are invested with religious attitudes, values, and assumptions which twenty-first century readers may find unfamiliar, perhaps even uncongenial. And yet the ability to grasp these poems, together with the understanding both of their religious attitudes and their aesthetic quality, probably depends as much as anything upon the degree of understanding, and even of sympathy, for these attitudes which the student can bring to his or her reading. It is useful to understand, for example, that the

Blessed Virgin Mary figured prominently in medieval religiousness (the object of devotion more often by men than by women, according to some scholars), as did issues like death (the dead are still present to the living in many texts), and persons like the saints (who had the power yet to inform the reader's life). More than anything, these poems both reveal and encode a perception of the deity that recognized Christ as God, while allowing as well for his humanity, so envisioning both him and his all-powerful Father in terms that are less personal, and usually more astringent, than is present in much contemporary religious discourse.

Such perceptions and attitudes were integral to everyday life, both religious and secular, and when met in the texts which follow, it is reasonable to consider their motion and effect. In addition, it is usually (though not always) a mistake to assume that there is a challenge to orthodoxy implied in departures from traditional practices, whether apparent or real. Traditionally, Rome has been slow to pronounce upon personal apprehensions of the divine, which sometimes are called private revelations, or to codify the vast majority of devotional, often extra-biblical, practices upon which certain of these revelations, and certain of the texts which follow, depend. But it is useful to consider the religious as well as the aesthetic issues involved in these poems, issues which they often either assume or reveal. It is only by doing so that the reader can come to an understanding of what these texts meant to those who wrote and those who first read them, and so grasp the inner, often religious life around which they were constructed and created. Religion and poetry are both finally concerned with that which is interior, not exterior, to persons.

This Edition

With a very few exceptions, I have selected lyrics for the main part of this edition whose authors are anonymous, though, as I have noted, I have placed, in two appendices, Appendix A and Appendix B, lyrics by Geoffrey Chaucer and by three important, but lesser known, poets, and three other lyrics, written by unnamed women authors, in Appendix C. I have separated these texts from the others because the lyrics, ballads, and carols printed here represent some of the best and most interesting poems in the medieval English tradition, though their distinctive voice, attitudes, and assumptions are now less familiar than they once were. Part of the interest, and also part of the challenge, in presenting an edition of Middle English lyrics concerns the nature and the extent of the editor's intervention. It would be a mistake in every case to present the poems exactly as they appear in manuscript, both because of the difficulties that would pose for the intended audience, and also because the poems presented here occur in many very different manuscripts, each with its own orthographic eccentricities, scribal practices, and outright mistakes.

But it seems to me no less mistaken to regularize and modernize every poem in exactly the same way, as if to imply that all of these poems were composed by the same poet and transcribed by the same scribe! Thus, although I have modernized letter forms, punctuation, capitalization, and line division throughout, I have generally preserved the orthographic irregularities which these texts present. Thus, I have preserved the first person singular pronoun as "Y/y" when it is so indicated in the manuscript, and have also preserved "y" as written within individual words. In certain of the longer poems I have occasionally and silently both supplied and (more rarely) cancelled "H/h," and have sometimes modernized both upper and lower case d/t, c/k, i/j, q/w and (though very rarely) u/v, where I thought the change might be helpful or even necessary for the student. Inevitably, this has led to occasional inconsistencies (the hobgoblin of little minds, according to Emerson), but as a general rule I have tried to preserve a sense of the ways in which these poems appear on the manuscript page, so as not entirely to obscure the sense of difference which appears between medieval and modern texts, whether written or printed.

Having thus kept something of the orthographic appearance of a late medieval English manuscript, albeit one whose accidentals have been modernized and which has been written only in the Roman alphabet, I have assumed a reader who has an interest in medieval lyric poetry, and is so prepared to accommodate changes in spelling, diction, and syntax. Such a reader will probably have enough knowledge of Middle English to understand that some irregularity is inevitable, and that all poems cannot possibly be expected to look or sound the same. It has been my experience that such students value a sense of the way lyrics actually appeared to their first readers, and do not invariably require a totalizing modernization of medieval texts. But I also have tried to be realistic, and in a very few cases I have simplified or modernized the spelling of common words, like *his*, *she*, *though*, and *us*, when I judged that the medieval orthography would confuse long before it would inform. For the same reason, I have generally and silently expanded contractions, and have employed side glosses throughout. Still, part of the interest of medieval manuscripts is their regular irregularity, the way in which, in matters of orthography, syntax, and presentation, they constantly show many hands and many minds at work.

Another part of the interest of these poems involves their context in the manuscripts which preserve them. It is quite true that many Middle English lyrics have come down to us only because they were written down more or less at random on blank spaces in manuscript leaves, often on the front or the back folios of the manuscript. But the choice of which lyric to inscribe on these free spaces was not always random. On the contrary, certain lyrics were written down because in one way or another their very presence served to comment on some or all of the works contained in the manuscript in which they were inscribed, and where this has seemed to me to be the case, I have indicated and discussed that circumstance in the headnote to the poem concerned.

Throughout, I have benefitted from consulting editions made before me, particularly those of Brown, Davies, Duncan, Gray, and Robbins, and these are listed in my Abbreviations. Because the notes to these editions retain particular interest for students, I have listed the numbers in each of these anthologies which correspond to the lyrics I have published here. I also have added general introductions to each section of poems, and more specific introductions, sometimes including bibliographical references, to each lyric, ballad, or carol, which I have included. Works listed in the bibliography are cited throughout the headnotes to the poems only in short form. Because the focus of this edition is on the student's reading of the lyrics and understanding of their context, I have in each case sought to engage the reader in questions which seem to me important in understanding the text, and although the bibliographical references I have included are not complete, I have listed what seem to me the more important and relevant studies. Other references are available in Rosemary Greentree's bibliography *The Middle English Lyric and Short Poem*, listed in my own bibliography, below. Extensive critical work, much of it relatively recent, has now made it possible to address each lyric, ballad, and carol as an individual work of art, which they indeed are, while re-maining alert to their larger contexts, too.

But I have tried as well to allow the religious and secular attitudes present in these texts to appear as directly as possible. Many of the poems which follow are admirable works of art in their own right, but certain of the religious poems, perhaps particularly those concerned with Christ's Passion, are best understood when their religious context is taken into account as well. A reader does not need to be a devout Christian thus to engage such poems, though equally religious faith is no bar to their interpretation, but in certain respects the religious aesthetic differs from the secular in that it either perceives or invests in Christ's life and death an intrinsic meaning which radiates out to inform all of creation. That is why even a short poem on Christ's Passion often encodes a significance greater than the text itself may seem to reveal, and why it was, and sometimes still is, potentially so powerful. It is thus often useful to read many of the poems which follow with an understanding of their symbolic as well as their manifest implications clearly in mind.

The very brevity of many Middle English lyrics can be deceptive. They are in fact rich and often very demanding works of art, but varied too, each with its own challenges, whether textual, interpretive, or both. Even the groupings I have imposed here can mislead as easily as they can inform, and it is important that the reader consider how, within each section, this poem differs from that one, and perhaps even reaches out to another group entirely.

Voice, Tone, and Intention

Three of the most important issues present in the study of medieval English lyrics concern the presence and mutual influence of voice, tone, and intention. "To stress voice in discussions of poetry may be simply a reminder of the large extent to which poetry depends on sound," avers the *Princeton Encyclopedia*.[21] And it is indeed a frequently layered voice that informs tone, itself often the most important, and sometimes the most difficult, aspect of any late medieval lyric. The word "voice" assumes a speaker, not necessarily the poet him- or herself, but one whose speech is informed by an understanding that gives meaning to his or her words, whether she or he be a cleric or a noble, an omniscient narrator or a failed protagonist, a devout Christian or an amorous lover. The speaker's tone, however, can be equally informed by far more individual details, past or present circumstances, and poetic or personal predispositions, and these often register expressively with the audience. Particularly in medieval lyrics, where performance, in one way or another, may often be assumed, the line between persona and poet can be thin indeed. In certain of the lyrics which follow, the poet's voice seems to emerge from meditation in order to address, as a reconstructed persona, an audience which is called upon to reflect, or to celebrate, or even to act, according to different, if sometimes indeterminate, circumstances.

Middle English lyrics, and particularly good ones, usually present an individual poetic voice, though to hear that voice at all clearly the reader must be very atten-tive indeed. The voices present in these lyrics reveal a variety of attitudes: devout and reflective, earnest and engaged, ecstatic and celebratory, irritated and caustic, to name only some of them. Sometimes the tone will inform, or even determine, a poem's meaning. "Maiden in the mor lay" (no. 20) has been read both as a secular dance song and as a poem at least originating in praise of Mary Magdalene, and though it is just possible that its meaning may shift from secular to sacred depending upon its use and context, it is harder to make the same argument with a poem like "Foweles in the frith" (no. 21), in which the reader's identification of the poem's tone will serve to fix the nature and extent of the speaker's pain or irony.

But voice can be informed by poetic intention, the nature of which, in any given poem, may only apparently be clear. Although it is true that Christian intention is present, directly or indirectly, in many lyrics, it is good to reflect on T. S. Eliot's warning in *The Use of Poetry and the Use of Criticism* (1933) that: "The 'experience' in question [in a poem] may be the result of feelings so numerous and ultimately so obscure in their origins, that even if there be communication of them, the poet may hardly be aware of what he was communicating; and what is there to be communicated was not in existence before the poem was completed." And even in these pre-modern lyrics, both meaning and intention sometimes still need to be negotiated. There are of course poems in which voice and tone are one, and together either inform, or are informed by, the poet's palpable intention. This circumstance sometimes exists in Middle English lyrics too, though more often the three interact complexly.

No doubt the fact that many religious lyrics were rooted (or at least began) in Christian teaching informed their authors' intention, but this teaching was neither simple nor univocal. When a poet wrote within the Christian tradition many possibilities were apparent, and she or he chose from them freely, according to what was, or seemed to be, indicated. Equally, when the poet drew upon scripture for his or her images and symbols, she or he often wrote in dialogue with some aspects of Christian tradition, so that it was the text which gave voice to the teaching, not the other way. Originality thus emerged from the departures the poet made from that tradition, from the changes she or he imposed upon it, and poetic voice, as much as Christian teaching, was what finally informed the poem. Thus, for example, in "Adam lay i-bowndyn" (no. 9), the poet rejects the usual teaching that Adam's sin was a *felix culpa*, or happy fault, because without it Christ would not have come to redeem humankind, in favor of a celebration of Mary – insisting that without Adam's sin Mary would not have become Queen of Heaven. In "I syng of a mayden that is makeles" (no. 13), the Blessed Virgin is represented as choosing the King of Kings (Christ) not as her lover, but, conflating traditions, for her son. It is not that the Middle English poet avoids intention, so much as that she or he is not finally constrained by the traditional orthodoxy with which it is sometimes, but wrongly, identified, and both views and treats it as adaptable, and even capable of change, according to the requirements of verse.

Voice, tone, and intention are thus present in most of the poems which follow, but their relationship can be complicated, in both secular lyrics and religious, by the circumstances which they address, and by the individual poetic identity upon which they depend. In these lyrics, voice, tone, and intention often attend upon each other, whether in opposition or in a kind of elaborate interchange which issues in dialogue, and creates a poem less from their separate properties than from their interaction. If intention holds out a variety of forms, assumptions, and attitudes, voice elects an opening, a narrative, and a theme, and together they issue in tone and movement both. Medieval lyrics fed upon each other, sometimes in imitation and extension, sometimes by a rejection of past narrative, and in a desire to make a new way. Above all they sought, like most performance art forms, to engage their audience, to move by language, to be heard.

Music

Music in the Middle Ages was both sacred and secular, and there was a pious belief that the particular form of sacred music known as Gregorian Chant had been divinely revealed to Pope Gregory I, called Gregory the Great (c.540–604, Pope 590–604), by the Holy Spirit. The sacredness and otherness of devout music has been brilliantly captured in an excellent musical project involving medieval lyrics at Mount Holyoke College in Massachusetts, directed by Margaret Switten, which has produced a recorded selection of Middle English lyrics and poems as part of a larger project, *The Medieval Lyric*, Anthology III, CD 5, together with an accompanying study by Howard D. Chickering, Jr., *Medieval English Lyric* (South Hadley, Mass.: Mount Holyoke College, 1989). There is a pioneering study by E. J. Dobson and F. Ll. Harrison, *Medieval English Songs* (London and Boston: Faber and Faber, 1979), which includes "words and music of all songs with English texts up to about 1400" (p. 11), and so lists textual commentary, modern instrumentation, and musical commentary for each of the songs printed, including: "Mirie it is while sumer i-last" (no. 2), pp. 121, 241, 297; "Svmer is i-cumen in" (no. 8), pp. 143, 246, 308; "Maiden in the mor lay" (no. 20), pp. 188, 269, and 306 together with the associated Latin hymn *Peperit virgo*, pp. 189, 270, 306; and "Foweles in the frith" (no. 21), pp. 142, 246, 299. There is an instructive review by Thomas G. Duncan in *Medium Aevum* 50 (1981): 338–41. See now Kristin Boklund-Lagopoulou, *"I have a yong suster": Popular Song and the Middle English Lyric* (Dublin: Four Courts Press, 2002).

Although not easily available, there are excellent photographs of the manuscript folios which contain music for four of the songs printed here, numbers 2, 21, 46, and 49, in J. F. R. and C. Stainer, *Early Bodleian Music: Sacred and Secular Songs Together with Other MS Compositions in the Bodleian Library, Oxford (1185–1505)* (London: Novello and Company, 1901), and other modern transcriptions of the music. See in vol. I: "Mirie it is while sumer i-last" (no. 2), plates II and III (vol. II, pp. 10–22); "Foweles in the frith"(no. 21), plate XV (vol. II, pp. 104–5); "Go day" (no. 46), plate XLVII (vol. II, p. 107); "Owre kynge went forth" (no. 49), plates LXVI–LXVII (vol. II, pp. 128–9). More readily available is a short book aimed at the general reader by Nicholas Bell, *Music in Medieval Manuscripts* (London: The British Library, 2001), which includes numerous color plates of neumed manuscript leaves, including one of British Library, London, Harley MS 978, folio 11 verso, which contains "Svmer is i-cumen in" (no. 8).

On medieval and medieval English music generally, see John Stevens, *Words and Music in the Middle Ages: Song, Narrative, Dance and Drama, 1050–1350* (Cambridge: Cambridge University Press, 1986); John Caldwell, *The Oxford History of English Music*, vol. I, *From the Beginnings to c.1715* (Oxford: Clarendon Press, 1991);

and two recent volumes in *The New Oxford History of Music* (New York: Oxford University Press): vol. II, Richard Crocker and David Hiley, eds., *The Early Middle Ages to 1300* (1990), and vol. III (i), Reinhard Strohm and Bonnie J. Blackburn, eds., *Music as Concept and Practice in the Late Middle Ages* (2001).

Notes

1   On the connection of the Middle English lyric to Old English poems see Seth Lerer, "The Genre of the Grave and the Origins of the Middle English Lyric," *Modern Language Quarterly* 58 (1997): 127–61, and Peter Dronke, "On the Continuity of the Middle English Love Lyric," in E. Chaney and P. Mack, eds., *England and the Continental Renaissance: Essays in Honour of J. B. Trapp* (Woodbridge: The Boydell Press, 1990), pp. 7–21, reprinted in P. Dronke, ed., *Latin and Vernacular Poets of the Middle Ages* (Hampshire and Brookfield, Vt.: Variorum, 1991), no. XII.

2   For an overview of the religious traditions which informed the development of the lyric, see Rita Copeland, "The Middle English 'Candet Nudatum Pectus' and the Norms of Early Vernacular Translation Practice," *Leeds Studies in English* NS 15 (1984): 57–81; Siegfried Wenzel, *Preachers, Poets and the Early English Lyric* (Princeton: Princeton University Press, 1986); and John Fleming, "The Friars and Medieval English Literature," in David Wallace, ed., *The Cambridge History of Medieval English Literature* (Cambridge: Cambridge University Press, 1999, reprinted 2002), pp. 349–75. For a history of the friars, C. H. Lawrence, *The Friars: The Impact of the Early Mendicant Movement on Western Society*, The Medieval World (London and New York: Longman, 1994), and on their opposition, Penn R. Szittya, *The Antifraternal Tradition in Medieval Literature* (Princeton: Princeton University Press, 1986). Lawrence has also written *Medieval Monasticism: Forms of Religious Life in Western Europe in the Middle Ages*, third edition, The Medieval World (London and New York: Longman, 2001), an attractive and informative introduction to medieval religious attitudes.

3   Henry Chadwick, *The Church in Ancient Society: From Galilee to Gregory the Great*, Oxford History of the Christian Church (Oxford and New York: Oxford University Press, 2001), p. 360. Boniface Ramsey OP notes that during the Arian crisis of 386 Ambrose's hymns "became famous as both a consolation and a kind of rallying cry for the faithful of Milan." He adds: "It is hard to know how many hymns Ambrose may have written, but his reputation was such that a fairly large number were ascribed to him, including the *Exsultet* and the *Te Deum* . . . It is probably the case that the bulk of Ambrose's hymnody has been lost." *Ambrose*, The Early Church Fathers (London and New York: Routledge, 1997), p. 65. Ramsey prints texts and translations of the four best authenticated of Ambrose's hymns, all of them referred to by Augustine, pp. 166–73. The full extent of the influence of Ambrose's hymns on Western music is hard to calculate.

4   On the famous passage in Pliny testifying to the presence of songs (possibly hymns) in early Christianity see A. N. Sherwin-White, *The Letters of Pliny: A Historical and Social Commentary* (Oxford: Clarendon Press, 1966), pp. 702–8. I cite Saint Augustine,

Confessions, trans. Henry Chadwick, The World's Classics (Oxford and New York: Oxford University Press, 1992), p. 165; Latin from the edition of James J. O'Donnell (Oxford: Clarendon Press, 1992), I, 109. Referring to the passage in the *Confessions* cited above (IX 7.15), O'Donnell remarks that Augustine "may be embroidering the events of 386 in memory for effect" (III, 110). No doubt congregational singing would have developed and spread in any case, but crises certainly can change practices, and that of 386 may well have been at very least an important precipitating factor. For the use and development of hymns in the early church see Wayne A. Meeks, *The First Urban Christians: The Social World of the Apostle Paul*, second edition (New Haven and London: Yale University Press, 2003), pp. 144–50. Throughout my treatment of the medieval lyric in these paragraphs I am indebted to Peter Dronke, *The Medieval Lyric*, third edition (Cambridge: D. S. Brewer, 1996), especially pp. 32 ff., where I first found the quote from Augustine cited above. But I have been informed as well by Dronke's *Medieval Latin and the Rise of European Love-Lyric*, 2 vols, second edition (Oxford: Clarendon Press, 1968), and his *Poetic Individuality in the Middle Ages: New Departures in Poetry 1000–1150*, second edition, Westfield Publications in Medieval Studies 1 (London: Westfield Press, 1986).

5   Peter Brown, *The Rise of Western Christendom: Triumph and Diversity*, AD 200–1000 second edition (Oxford: Blackwell, 2003), p. 187. Brown suggests that such ecclesiastical music became one of several cultural indicators which were both a product of, and contributed to a "more deeply felt basis of communal identity" than any available from a more secular source. The effects on the laity were pronounced. "They were fellow believers. They were no longer fellow citizens." Within a century of Justinian's death, "the populations of Egypt and Syria, having fallen under Muslim rule, would forget that they had ever lived under a Christian empire" (p. 189). Church music alone did not create this effect, but it was (and remains) a most powerful force in defining attitudes and reenforcing values.

6   J. A. Westrup, "Medieval Song," in Dom Anselm Hughes, ed., *Early Medieval Music Up to 1300. New Oxford History of Music*, 2 (Oxford: Oxford University Press, 1955), p. 237. Bernart's great power is to invest the conventions of love with extraordinary and felt power. See, among many commentators, L. T. Topsfield, *Troubadours and Love* (Cambridge: Cambridge University Press, 1975), pp. 111–36.

7   For a survey of the field see Dronke, *The Medieval Lyric* (see note 4 above), and also Patrick S. Diehl, *The Medieval European Religious Lyric: An Ars Poetica* (Berkeley, Los Angeles, and London: University of California Press, 1985), and two valuable and relevant chapters in W. F. Bolton, ed., *The Penguin History of Literature*, vol. 1, *The Middle Ages*, revised edition (Harmondsworth: Penguin Books, 1986) – Rosemary Woolf, "Later Poetry: The Popular Tradition," pp. 267–311, and Douglas Gray, "Later Poetry: The Courtly Tradition," pp. 313–67.

8   Dronke, *The Medieval Lyric*, pp. 184–5. The name of the evidently imaginative notary who inserted the lyrics into his register in 1286 was Nicholaus Phylippi.

9   On this connection see Winthrop Wetherbee, "The Place of the Secular Latin Lyric," in William D. Paden, ed., *Medieval Lyric: Genres in Historical Context*, Illinois Medieval Series (Urbana and Chicago: University of Illinois Press, 2000), pp. 95–125.

An historical and critical study of both the Latin tradition and of certain of its modern critics. There is a like study of the medieval English lyric by Julia Boffey, "Middle English Lyrics: Texts and Interpretations," in Tim William Machan, ed., *Medieval Literature: Texts and Interpretation*, Texts and Studies, vol. 79 (Binghamton, N.Y.: Medieval and Renaissance Texts and Studies, 1991), pp. 121–38.

10   See David L. Jeffrey, *The Early English Lyric and Franciscan Spirituality* (Lincoln, Nebr.: University of Nebraska Press, 1975), which has however been subjected to severe criticism by Caroline Walker Bynum, in *Medievalia et Humanistica* NS 7 (1976): 195–7 and by Edward Wilson, in the *Review of English Studies* NS 7 (1976): 318–21, in particular for failing to clarify what the phrase "Franciscan spirituality" actually denotes. But see too Rossell Hope Robbins, "The Authors of Middle English Religious Lyrics," *Journal of English and Germanic Philology* 39 (1940): 230–8, and Fleming, "The Friars and Medieval English Literature" (see note 2 above), which also argue for an important Franciscan role in the creation of the Middle English lyric.

11   On the role of Latin sermons, Siegfried Wenzel, "The English Verses in the *Fasciculus Morum*," in Beryl Rowland, ed., *Chaucer and Middle English Studies in Honor of Rossell Hope Robbins* (London: Allen & Unwin, 1974), pp. 230–48, and on the Prymer, Alexandra Barratt, "The Prymer and its Influence on Fifteenth-Century English Passion Lyrics," *Medium Aevum* 44 (1975): 264–79.

12   For a good case study, see the discussion in Peter Dronke, "Two Thirteenth-Century Religious Lyrics," in Beryl Rowland, ed., *Chaucer and Middle English Studies in Honor of Rossell Hope Robbins* (London: Allen & Unwin, 1974), pp. 392–406, reprinted in P. Dronke, ed., *The Medieval Poet and his World*, Raccolta di Studi e Testi 164 (Rome: Edizioni de Storia e Letteratura, 1964), pp. 341–56. The issue is also addressed in two books of great importance for the study of the Middle English religious lyric, Rosemary Woolf, *The English Religious Lyric in the Middle Ages* (Oxford: Clarendon Press, 1968), *passim*, and in Douglas Gray, *Themes and Images in the Medieval English Religious Lyric* (London and Boston: Routledge & Kegan Paul, 1972), pp. 59–71.

13   On the role of the Franciscans in the development of the Middle English lyric, see Jeffrey, *The Early English Lyric* and Robbins, "The Authors of Middle English Religious Lyrics" (see note 10 above). On Herebert see Stephen R. Reimer, ed., *The Works of William Herebert, OFM*, Studies and Texts 81 (Toronto: Pontifical Institute of Medieval Studies, 1987); his poems appear on pp. 111–38. John Audelay's poems have been edited by Ella K. Whiting, *The Poems of John Audelay*, EETS 184 (1931); see too Eric Stanley, "The Verse Forms of Jon the Blynde Awdelay," in Helen Cooper and Sally Mapstone, eds., *The Long Fifteenth Century: Essays for Douglas Gray* (Oxford: Clarendon Press, 1997), pp. 99–121. Rolle's English poems have been edited by Hope Emily Allen, *English Writings of Richard Rolle Hermit of Hampole* (Oxford: Clarendon Press, 1931); his poems appear on pp. 37–53.

14   Sarah McNamer, "Female Authors, Provincial Settings: The Re-versing of Courtly Love in the Findern Manuscript," *Viator* 22 (1991): 279–310. The article contains an edition of the poems which McNamer finds to have been written by women in

an appendix, 302–10. There are other lyrics written by women printed in Alexandra Barratt, ed., *Women's Writing in Middle English*, Longman Annotated Texts (London and New York: Longman, 1992), pp. 262–300. On women's reading see Mary C. Erler, *Women, Reading and Piety in Late Medieval England*, Cambridge Studies in Medieval Literature (Cambridge: Cambridge University Press, 2002).

15 On the association of Middle English lyrics and the English court see Rossell Hope Robbins, "The Middle English Court Love-Lyric," in W. T. H. Jackson, ed., *The Interpretation of Medieval Lyric Poetry* (New York: Columbia University Press, 1980), pp. 205–32, and Richard Firth Greene, *Poets and Princepleasers: Literature and the English Court in the Late Middle Ages* (Toronto, Buffalo, and London: Toronto University Press, 1980), especially chapter 3, "A Lettered Court," pp. 71–100.

16 Both are paper manuscripts. MS Sloane 2593 now contains only 37 folios (folio 2 had previously been numbered 49), and measures $5\frac{7}{8}$ inches by $4\frac{3}{8}$ inches; Balliol College, Oxford MS 354 contains 256 folios, and measures $11\frac{1}{2}$ by $4\frac{1}{2}$ inches. Sloane 2593 is preserved in a serviceable modern board; Balliol 354 retains its original limp vellum binding. They are described, along with other collections also containing carols, in Richard Leighton Green, ed., *The Early English Carols* (see Abbreviations), pp. 306–7 and 320–1, and Hill's background has been examined in William P. Hills, "Richard Hill of Hillend and Balliol MS 354," *Notes and Queries* 177 (1939): 352–6. Both manuscripts are further discussed in Kristin Boklund-Lagopoulou, *"I have a yong suster": Popular Song and the Middle English Lyric* (Dublin: Four Courts Press, 2002), pp. 63–86 and 202–33. On Hill's religious lyrics see Julia Boffey, " 'Loke on this wrytyng man, for thi devocion!': Focal Texts in Some Later Middle English Religious Lyrics," in O. S. Pickering, ed., *Individuality and Achievement in Middle English Poetry* (Cambridge: D. S. Brewer, 1997), pp. 129–45.

17 This point is made in one of the best treatments of the Middle English secular lyric, Julia Boffey, *Manuscripts of English Courtly Love Lyrics in the Later Middle Ages*, Manuscript Studies 1 (Cambridge: D. S. Brewer, 1985), p. 58. But see too Boffey's chapters on "Authorship and Composition," pp. 61–86, "Currency and Transmission," pp. 87–112, and "Readers and Owners of the Manuscripts," pp. 113–41, in the same study. See also Arthur K. Moore, *The Secular Lyric in Middle English* (Lexington: University of Kentucky Press, 1951), for another account of these lyrics, which offer opportunities for further study.

18 Robin Hood songs, tales, and ballads are legion, and deserve all the attention they have received. Still useful is R. B. Dobson and John Taylor, eds., *Rymes of Robin Hood: An Introduction to the English Outlaw* (London: Heinemann; Pittsburgh: University of Pittsburgh Press, 1976), though its texts should now be supplemented by Stephen Knight, ed., *Robin Hood: The Forresters Manuscript. British Library Additional 71158* (Cambridge: D. S. Brewer, 1998), and by Knight's *Robin Hood: A Complete Study of the English Outlaw* (Oxford: Blackwell, 1994). On the literary background see too Jess B. Bessinger, "The *Gest of Robin Hood* Revisited," in Larry D. Benson, ed., *The Learned and the Lewed* (Cambridge, Mass.: Harvard University Press, 1974), pp. 355–69, and Douglas Gray, "The Robin Hood Poems," *Poetica* 18 (1984): 1–39; on the historical background (and *contra* Knight) see: John Bellamy, *Robin Hood: An*

Historical Enquiry (London and Sydney: Croom Helm, 1985); J. C. Holt, *Robin Hood*, revised edition (London: Thames and Hudson, 1990); Maurice Keen, *The Outlaws of Medieval England*, revised edition (London: Routledge, 1977); and J. C. Maddicott, "The Birth and Setting of the Ballads of Robin Hood," *English Historical Review* 93 (1978): 276–99. There was a lively exchange in *Past and Present* involving R. H. Hilton, "The Origins of Robin Hood," 14 (1958): 30–44; Keen, "Robin Hood – Peasant or Gentleman?" 19 (1961): 7–15; and Holt, "The Origins and Audience of the Ballads of Robin Hood," 18 (1960): 89–110, and 19 (1961): 16–18.

19 On the American ballads see in particular *The Ballad Book of John Jacob Niles* (Boston: Houghton Mifflin, 1960, reprinted New York: Dover, 1970), which contains the American versions of the ballads I have printed here.

20 On further connections between carols and lyrics see a pioneering essay by Douglas Gray, "Fifteenth-century Lyrics and Carols," in Helen Cooney, ed., *Nation, Court and Culture: New Essays on Fifteenth-century Poetry* (Dublin: Four Courts Press, 2001), pp. 168–83, which, *inter alia*, newly remarks the extent to which autobiographical experience can figure in these texts, the ways in which the carol reflects topics also present in the fifteenth-century lyric, and why it is that many carols fall outside the traditional categories assigned to them.

21 Alex Preminger and T. V. F. Brogan, eds., *The New Princeton Encyclopedia of Poetry and Poetics* (Princeton, N.J.: Princeton University Press, 1993), *s.v.* "Voice," "Tone," and "Intention." I am indebted to the *Princeton Encyclopedia* for the allusions to and quotations from Eliot I have cited, and for informing the discussion which follows.

I

Poems of Mourning, Fear, and Apprehension

This anthology opens with a late fifteenth-century devotional poem which offers an insight into the state of mind which religious lyrics were calculated at once to induce and to assume in their readers, a state of mind which involved a vivid calling to mind ("a remembering") of Christ's passion, combined with a felt reflection upon past sins. This combination was powerful and effective, and recurs often throughout the period within which these lyrics were written, though it is frequently combined with a plea for God's mercy. The very earliest Middle English lyrics, on the other hand, often present two very real, if primarily lexical, problems as well. First, thirteenth-century English is difficult to read, so that even when we know what a word means we do not necessarily know what connotations or implications it may have had for a contemporary reader, though it is often possible to guess. Second, it is sometimes not easy to know whether the poem we are reading is secular or religious. In the past, any expression of love was thought to refer to secular love, with the poem narrated by one who seemed to be in agony over a love affair gone wrong, or at least in danger of doing so. During the late 1960s these earlier readings were revised, and early poetry was viewed as all but universally religious, though the nature of the religious insight they offered often was understood in very different ways. What emerges most clearly, however, is the degree to which self-reflection, and what can reasonably be called philosophical meditation, figured in several of the earliest compositions. Just as it was naive earlier to assume that any poem which spoke of love and suffering was a love lyric, so it was no less mistaken to attribute that suffering to such commonplaces as the existence of an old law which Christ would change, or a putatively universal fear of final judgment.

A sense of foreboding runs through some of the lyrics in this first section, creating a sense of personal loss which is attributed less to that individual's (or to Adam's) sin, than to an uncertainty concerning the way the universe has been constructed, and the place of human beings in it. These concerns appear explicitly in some later medieval lyrics, like no. 19 below, but they are present, explicitly and implicitly, in the early period, too. In some ways the mentalities which emerge from these lyrics echo those which appear from time to time in the *Ecclesiastical History of the English People* which the Venerable Bede completed in 731 AD. In Book II chapter 13 of that work, Bede tells of the response in 627 to the Christian missionary Paulinus by one of the chief men of the pagan King Edwin of Bernicia. Life seemed to him like a winter feast, during which a sparrow flew swiftly in one door and out another, through the hall where men were making merry. While in the hall, the bird, like living persons, experienced a moment of calm and even security, but out in the winter night again all was lost. This same sense of doubt and fear, against which the new Christian faith offered an explanation and a bulwark, appears in some of these lyrics, but certain of them preserve as well a sense of recent apprehension, a feeling that though all may yet be well it is not so yet, and that there are important choices to be made. There is no Christian triumphalism in these verses, and what certainty there is seems often to be conditional. Instead, the poems seem sprung from a philosophical reflection upon the impermanence of the world around us, on the contradictions between nature and history, on the potentially meaningful but difficult to understand consolations that religion offers, and on the integrity necessary to lead the Christian to confront the choices which are his fate.

1

IMEV 2442. Bodleian Library, Oxford. MS Douce 1 (*SC* 21575), fol. 54v. Brown C no. 143.

Originally placed as an introduction to a group of Latin and English prayers and English religious lyrics, this late medieval poem was intended to introduce a prayerful state of mind in its medieval reader, and can serve even today to show modern students how many of these lyrics were read – not simply aesthetically, though there is a religious aesthetic present in their composition, but devoutly, so that the image of Christ's Passion, when fixed in the mind, could inform the will, and permit contemplation to direct the imagination. It speaks as well to one form of anxiety which, though not always stated as such, is often assumed, and that is a sense that the actions of this life will determine the Christian's salvation. But like many religious lyrics, this one finally offers assurance rather than condemnation, and seeks to encourage the reader to call to mind Christ's Passion, to consider its implications, and then to take up the teachings it offers.

The "arms of the passion" refers to the *Arma Christi*, an often dramatic narrative and meditative prayer poem identifying each of the instruments associated with Christ's Passion which I have printed elsewhere from the manuscript containing this poem, MS Douce 1, a tiny devotional manuscript measuring approximately 2″ by 2¾″ and containing 82 folios. Douce 1 also includes an associated poem on Christ's blood, and both appear in my study, "Two English Devotional Poems of the Fifteenth Century," *Notes and Queries* 213 (1968): 4–11. Related poems in the same group are on Christ's Five Wounds, printed by Douglas Gray, ibid. 208, NS 10 (1963): 50–1, 82–9, 126–34, 163–8; and on the Virgin, which appears in Brown C no. 44.

O Glorius God, redemer of mankynde,
Whiche on the crosse hyng full of compassyon,   *hyng = hung*
Graunt of thi grace, within my herte and mynde,
Holly to remember the armes of thy passion.   *Holly = wholly*

Enrote, good lorde, thi greuous paynes strong,   *Enrote = fix, establish*
Depe in my thought, auoydynge all synne,
And purge the vyces that hathe ben in me longe,
With contrite herte these verses to begynne.

Enclyne, alowe, of mercy now thyne ere,
Contemplynge thy paynes, vnto my peticion,
And graunt me grace so to serue the here,
Affter this lyfe to be in thi tuycion. Amen.   *tuycion = protection*

2

IMEV 2163. Bodleian Library, Oxford. Rawlinson MS G. 22 (*SC* 14755), fol. 1v. Brown A no. 7. Davies no. 2. Duncan A no. 36.

A long night suggesting the first traces of a thirteenth-century northern European winter, together with winds and stormy weather, figure as objective correlatives for the speaker's penitential state of mind. The manuscript also contains music, further complicating its meaning by suggesting that the song engaged its audience, and that that may have been its intention, though there was clearly a larger, more devout purpose implied as well. Voice matters here. Is the barely indicated coming of spring symbolic of a personal or, in our fallen world, of a spiritual rebirth? Or should we simply accept that the song, its music, and its splendidly realized psychological state of mind are all, at this point, that we can reasonably expect to know? The poem has been discussed widely, including in Raymond Oliver, *Poems Without Names: The English Lyric, 1200–1500* (1970) and Edmund Reiss, *The Art of the Middle English Lyric: Essays in Criticism* (1972), but still retains its mystery.

Mirie it is while sumer i-last	*sumer = springtime; ilast = lasts*
With fugheles song.	*fugheles = fowls', birds'*
Oc nu necheth windes blast	*Oc nu = but now; necheth = draws near*
And weder strong.	*weder strong = stormy weather*
Ej! Ej! What, this night is long!	*is = MS omission*
And Ich, with wel michel wrong,	*Ich = I; michel = much*
Soregh, and murne, and fast.	*Soregh = sorrow; murne = mourn*

3

IMEV 2320. Bodleian Library, Oxford. MS Arch. Selden, supra 74 (*SC* 3462), fol. 55v, col. 2. Brown A no. 1. Davies no. 6. Duncan A no. 84. Gray no. 21.

This is a poem in which tone and voice are everything. It is preserved in the Anglo-Norman version of the popular meditative companion *Speculum Ecclesiae* of St. Edmund of Abingdon, Archbishop of Canterbury (d. 1240), and places at its center the narrator's psychological and penitential state of mind, and so also that of the meditative reader. Notice the puns on "wod," which can mean "wood," "woods," and because the cross was made of wood, the cross on which Christ was crucified; and also the pun on "rode," which can mean both face and cross. The words both rhyme, and so play off each other allusively, wholly engaging the meditative reader.

The poem is easy to memorize and to recall, and probably had a very wide circulation indeed, both written and oral. It survives in numerous Latin, French, and English manuscripts, and may well have been recited daily by many intent Christians, clerical and lay, at the close of day. Its mindfulness is reflected in its evocation, at evening, of nature, as the reader takes some responsibility, because of sin, for Christ's Passion, and for the pain that Passion caused his mother Mary. The language is taut, seriously playful, and allusive, and mixes natural and scriptural imagery both easily and powerfully. The poem has been discussed widely, including in Douglas Gray, *Themes and Images in the Medieval English Religious Lyric* (1972) and Oliver, *Poems Without Names* (1970), and even today can catch up and involve the thoughtful reader.

Nou goth sonne vnder wod,   *goth* = goes; *sonne* = sun; *wod* = pun: *forest/cross*
Me reweth, Marie, thi faire rode.   *Me reweth* = I pity; *rode* = pun: *face/cross*
Nou goth sonne vnder tre,   *tre* = pun: *tree/cross*
Me reweth, Marie, thy sone and the.   *sone* = son

4

IMEV 1422. British Library, London. Arundel MS 292, fol. 3v. Brown A no. 13. Duncan A no. 43.

This is a poem at once easy to grasp and difficult to understand: easy to grasp because its surface meaning is intended to reach its reader quickly, difficult to understand because, try as we will, certain humane, psychological, and devout aspects of late medieval spirituality will forever remain closed to us. Notice the pointed reminder that, after death, bodies in the medieval period were often removed from the bed and placed on the floor; indeed there was a monastic practice of lifting a dying monk onto the floor even before he was dead, so that he could die lying upon sackcloth and ashes. But the poem warns that in some cases the descent to the floor reflects the even greater descent to Hell itself. Yet notice too the apparent reasonableness and confidence of the narrative voice, which is not greatly concerned with the unspoken threat of Hell, since if we attend to what we need to, that threat will not concern us.

This poem and the next one, together with nos 27 and 28 below, work as warning prayers which refer indirectly to the Signs of Death, and were both popular and largely private. This one appears in many late medieval manuscripts. Taken together, they give a fair insight into the assumptions, attitudes, and practices present in late medieval religious lyrics. There are two sometimes neglected early studies by Rossell Hope Robbins which describe such prayer-poems well, "Popular Prayers in Middle English Verse," *Modern Philology* 36 (1939): 337–50, and "Private Prayers in Middle English Verse," *Studies in Philology* 36 (1939): 466–75. There is a good treatment of medieval British death practices in Christopher Daniell, *Death and Burial in Medieval England, 1066–1550* (London: Routledge, 1997).

If man him bithocte	*bithocte = considered, bethought*
Inderlike and ofte,	*Inderlike = reflectively; ofte = often*
Hu arde is te fore	*Hu arde = how hard; te fore = the journey*
Fro bedde te flore,	*te flore = to floor*
Hu reuful is te flitte	*te flitte = the departing*
Fro flore te pitte,	*te pitte = to hell*
Fro pitte te pine	*te pine = to suffering, to lamentation*
That neure sal fine,	*fine = finish*
I wene non sinne	*wene = know; non = no; sinne = sin*
Sulde his herte winne!	*sulde = should; winne = win*

5

IMEV 4044. Trinity College, Cambridge. MS 323, fol. 47v. Brown A no. 30. Duncan A no. 45. Gray no. 84.

Notice the difference in voice between this poem, and no. 4, above. Rosemary Woolf, who was particularly sensitive to the psychological and cultural power of short, religious poems, remarks that it has "the sting and force of an epigram" and that it "contrasts the smallness and poverty of the grave" to the "splendor enjoyed by the dead man when he was alive" (*The English Religious Lyric in the Middle Ages*, 1968: 82). But, even though "winning the world" may have been more often charged against men than women, gender is curiously ambiguous, and what matters is that any form of prosperity is precarious and passing, and will not survive the grave. The question posed at the end suggests an even broader questioning, and the poem as a whole has a considered and unsettling edge to it.

Wen the turuf is thi tuur   *turuf = turf; tuur = tower*
And thi put is thi bour,   *put = grave; bour = inner chamber, bedroom*
Thi wel and thi wite throte   *wel = skin; wite = white*
Sulen wormes to note.   trans. = *Shall benefit worms*
Wat helpit thee thenne
Al the worilde wnne?   *worilde wnne = world's delight*

6

IMEV 375. Bodleian Library, Oxford. MS Eng. poet. e.1 (*SC* 29734), fol. 38v–39. Greene no. 370A.

Taken, often uncritically, as representative of late medieval religious attitudes generally, the *timor mortis* ("fear of death") poems and carols had a certain currency, and there is an excellent example by the notable Scots poet William Dunbar ("I that in heill wes, and gladnes"). In theme and tone *timor mortis* poems seem to the modern ear to echo the still familiar late medieval "Dance of Death," which showed the power of Death over the social classes. Death makes all persons follow him dancing, as he leads them away forever. Particularly in England, the *timor mortis* theme was sometimes associated with members of the clergy, whose voice can sometimes be heard, if dimly, in the background. Partly as a result, it was only rarely gendered (it is not here), though on its own the Dance of Death made its way into the nobility, and there is one well-known fifteenth-century Dance from France which is dedicated to women. Douglas Gray has published three sixteenth-century epitaphs which contain lines from the refrain of the English poem printed here (*Notes and Queries* 205 (1960): 403–4), to which Greene has added a fourth, and together these semi-public texts indicate that the poem and the sentiment both enjoyed a certain form of currency. Still, such texts were both conventional and (to some extent at least) confined by class, though this medieval poem retains a freshness and an energy which, at least in tone, seem almost to work against the text's explicit meaning. This poem, and others in its tradition, have been widely discussed, including in Woolf, *The English Religious Lyric in the Middle Ages* (1968). On the gendering of Death see Ann Tukey Harrison with Sandra L. Hindman, eds., *The Dance Macabre of Women* (Kent, Ohio and London: Kent State University Press, 1994).

In what estate soeuer I be,
Timor mortis conturbat me.　　　　　　trans. = fear of death terrifies me

As I went in a mery mornyng,
I hard a byrd bothe wep and syng,　　　　*hard = heard; byrd = bird*
Thys was the tenowr of her talkyng:　　　*tenowr = tenor, direction*
Timor mortis conturbat me.

I asked that byrd what sche ment,
"I am a musket bothe fayer and gent,　　　*musket = a male sparrowhawk*
For dred of deth I am al schent,　　　　　*schent = destroyed, punished*
Timor mortis conturbat me.

"Whan I schal dey, I know no day,   *dey = die*
What countre or place I cannot sey,
Wherfor this song syng I may,
Timor mortis conturbat me.

"Iesu Cryst, whane he schuld dey,
To hys Fader he gan sey,
'Fader,' he seyd, 'in Trinyte,
Timor mortis conturbat me.'"

Al Crysten pepull, behold and se,   *pepull = people*
This world is but a vanyte,
And replet with necessyte,   *replet = filled*
Timor mortis conturbat me.

Wak I or sclep, ete or drynke,   *sclep = sleep*
Whan I on my last end do thynk,
For grete fer my sowle do shrynke,   *fer = fear*
Timor mortis conturbat me.

God graunte vs grace hym for to serue,
And be at owr end whan we sterue,   *sterue = die*
And frome the fynd he vs preserue,   *fynd = devil, fiend*
Timor mortis conturbat me.

7

Worcester Cathedral MS Q. 46, fol. 229.

First published by Siegfried Wenzel, "Unrecorded Middle English Verses," *Anglia* 92 (1974): 55–78; the text cited below is on p. 73. This poem has a known Latin source, which begins "Si tibi magna domus, si splendida mensa, quid inde," in Hans Walther, ed., *Initia carminum ac versuum medii aevi latinorun* (Gottingen, 1959), no. 18017. The thirteenth-century manuscript was written by John Dumbleton, monk of Worcester, and its medieval foliation, which is in arabic, places the lyric on 238. The poem presents a proverbial variation on the very popular *ubi sunt* ("Where have they gone?") theme, though the tone and the sweep of this English translation is so powerful that the poet seems to have pressed his (very Western) theme so far that nothing remains of value. This was an aspect of the Christian *contemptus mundi* ("contempt for the world") which is sometimes difficult to understand since the sentiments which emerge in such poems cannot be easily differentiated, and can come to look at once identical and conventional.

In some cases such poems can best be understood by comparing the kinds of detachment they both describe and encode with those which lie outside of the Christian tradition. Thus, for example, the powerful rejection of the world present in this lyric can be set against the first of Buddha's "Four Noble Truths," which teaches that life is *dukkha*, where *dukkha* means something unsatisfactory and so finally empty, a view of life which orthodox Christianity usually rejects, but which this poem largely approves. The difference between these two teachings emerges in Buddha's second noble truth, which teaches that the origin of this sense of emptiness or imperfection lies in desire, and that desire upon the mistaken idea that objects are eternal. This poem's teaching and tone, on the other hand, are ascetic and astringent, and all but assert that life is finally without meaning – unless you see deeper, and with the eyes of faith. The inner reflection which such poems both assumed and called forth was thus often powerful and affecting. For Buddhist texts known (but unrecognized as such) to late medieval English readers see "Buddhism and Spirituality in Medieval England," in my *The Boundaries of Faith: The Development and Transmission of Medieval Spirituality*, Studies in the History of Christian Thought, volume LXVII (Leiden, New York, Cologne: E. J. Brill, 1996), pp. 31–46.

Thegh thou habbe casteles and toures	*Thege = although; habbe = have; toures = towers*
Halles, chaumbres, semeliche boures,	*semeliche = pleasing; boures = (private) rooms*
Wat therfore?	*Wat = what*

Theght thou habbe a fayr wyf
   and children fele,
Thy wille of al this worldes wele,
Wat therfore?

Theght = MS thetht = though; fele = fair

wele = weal, riches, possessions

Theght thou habbe haughte and erf,
Many men to serf,
Wat therfore?

haughte and erf = meadows and cattle

to serf = to serve (you)

Theght thou pase alle othere in schile,
Wyth worldes wisdam and flesches wil,
Wat therfore?

schile = skill, especially in reasoning

flesches wil = physical enjoyment

Thegh hap the lefte into heuene,
Aboven alle othere wit mannes steuene,
Wat therfore?

hap the lefte = chance lifts you

mannes steuene = human constitution

Al hyt passeyth and forgoth.
That furst was lef, hyt waxeth loth.
And therefore nought therfore.

trans. = everything passes and disappears

lef = dear; waxeth = grows; loth = hateful

trans. = and therefore (give) nothing for it

II

Poems of Joy and Celebration

The name originally assigned to Dante's great poem was not the *"Divine Comedy,"* but simply the *"Commedia."* The purpose of Christianity, finally, was to bring hope into the world, and with it joy. It was for that reason, among others, that Dante's poem ends, rather than begins, in Paradise. Faith has an end and a reward. To those who understand and believe, this world can surrender a higher meaning, even though that meaning is often obscure, and sometimes resists our understanding, at least while we are alive. But things are not an end in themselves – nor are people, nor even is love. Human love reflects, or at least can reflect, divine love, God's love for his people and for his church, and their love for him.

Yet in spite of its extraordinary ends, Christian celebration is not altogether unambiguous. "Our hearts are restless until they rest in Thee," Augustine wrote to and of God, reminding his readers of the uncertainty and incompleteness which is equally a part of all human lives, Christian or not. Thus celebration is often undertaken against a backdrop which includes sin and death, waiting and incompleteness, loneliness and expectation. But the celebration, even when it finally celebrates only the realization of joy to come, is real enough, and reflects a view of the universe which privileges the continuity of the natural world, the feasts and celebrations which make up the Christian one, and human wonder at divine Incarnation, which is at the bottom of it all.

Still, and especially for the student of medieval poetry, it is possible to take laughter, joy, and celebration too seriously. At least as important as Augustine are the many secular practices which attached to local, city, and national occasions, and the celebrations of great (and not so great) events and feast days, which came to define what has been called "the ritual year." These included bonfires and greenery, dancing and drama, bells and feasting, and which celebrated – often in a very secular way – holy days and other festivals. In the course of these celebrations, figures of Robin Hood, the Lord of Misrule, and mummers all played their part, and this particular aspect of late medieval England was one that the sixteenth-century Reformation took pains to address, attack, and sometimes to adapt. See among many studies, Ronald Hutton, *The Rise and Fall of Merry England: The Ritual Year 1400–1700* (Oxford and New York: Oxford University Press, 1994), especially pp. 5–48. There was also, of course, the simple human capacity to enjoy life, the change of seasons, and feasts like Christmas, and to do so even when times were hard.

8

IMEV 3223. British Library, London. Harley MS 978, fol. 11v. Brown A no. 6. Davies no. 3. Duncan A no. 110.

The following text is a *reverdie*, this one a partsong not uncommon in the late medieval period, which celebrates the return of spring with a display of natural imagery that seems to call forth the new season. It is uniquely preserved in a thirteenth-century manuscript very probably written between 1240 and 1260 by the monks of Reading Abbey, and includes both music and Latin instructions for singing, but these may be later than the song itself, and so indicate only how it was later performed. Still, at some point in its past, the poem has been identified as a *rota*, and as such was sung by six voices which entered one at a time in succession, the first such English song known to have been thus performed.

It has been widely discussed musicologically, including by Manfred F. Bukofzer, " 'Sumer Is Icumen In,' A Revision," *University of California Publications in Music* 2 (1944): 79–114, and by the notable musicologist Nino Perrotta, "On the Problem of 'Sumer Is Icumen In,' " *Musica Disciplina* 2 (1948): 205–16, though the dating discussion was effectively concluded by B. Schofield, "The Provenance and Date of 'Sumer is Icumen in,' " *Music Review* 9 (1948): 81–6. See further Jacques Handschin, "The Summer Canon and its Background," *Musica Disciplina* 33 (1949): 55–94, and Richard Crocker, "Polyphony in England in the Thirteenth Century," in Richard Crocker and David Hiley, eds., *The New Oxford History of Music: The Early Middle Ages to 1300* (New York: Oxford University Press, 1990), pp. 679–720, especially 712–14. There is a recent modern transcription of the song in John Caldwell, *The Oxford History of English Music* (Oxford: Clarendon Press, 1991) I, p. 61. Its specific literary and other qualities have been examined by Karin Boklund-Lagopoulou, *"I have a yong suster": Popular Song and the Middle English Lyric* (2002), Oliver, *Poems Without Names* (1970), and Reiss, *The Art of the Middle English Lyric* (1972). The folio which uniquely preserves the poem (see figure 1, p. 36) has been reproduced often, most recently in Nicholas Bell, *Music in Medieval Manuscripts* (London: British Library, 2001), p. 27.

Sing cuccu nu, sing cuccu!	*nu = now*
Sing cuccu, sing cuccu nu!	

Svmer is i-cumen in!	*Svmer = spring; is i-cumen = has come*
Lhude sing cuccu!	*Lhude = loud*
Groweth sed and bloweth med,	*sed = seed; bloweth = flowers; med = meadow*
And springeth the wode nu!	*springeth = springs (to life); wode = woods*

Figure 1 British Library MS Harley 978, folio 11v. This manuscript folio contains the famous and still often performed medieval *rota* "Summer [Spring] is i-cumen in" (no. 8), which is contained in this miscellaneous collection of music, medical treatises, and poetry, written in Reading toward the middle of the thirteenth century.

Sing cuccu nu . . .

Ewe bleteth after lomb,
Lhouth after calue, cu,   *Lhouth = lows; cu = cow*
Bulluc sterteth, bucke   *sterteth = leaps; bucke = stag or he-goat;*
    uerteth,   *uerteth = farts(?)*
Murie sing cuccu!

Sing cuccu nu . . .

Cuccu! Cuccu!
Wel singes thou, Cuccu!
Ne swik thu nauer nu!   *swik = stop, fail; nauer = never*

Sing cuccu nu . . .

9

IMEV 117 British Library, London. Sloane MS 2593, fol. 11. Brown C no. 83. Davies no. 71. Duncan A no. 108. Gray no. 2.

See figure 2, p. 39. This brilliant little poem turns on a theological teaching concerning Adam's sin, the *felix culpa* ("happy fault") which caused him to disobey God and eat the apple (itself a pun: in Latin *malum* means apple; *malus* means bad). The tree from which Adam's apple was picked was sometimes contrasted with the "tree" on which Christ was crucified; it was believed that they literally stood on the same spot. In some late medieval and early modern paintings, Christ's blood is represented as flowing down the cross and touching a skull (Adam's) which lies at its foot, baptizing it, and thus vividly linking Christ's redemptive Passion to Adam's sin. Adam's fault is thus "happy" because it caused Christ to manifest his love and become man in order to save humankind – but here the poet has brilliantly recast that commonplace idea to say instead that the great good which came from Adam's sin was that Mary became Queen of Heaven.

There has been much discussion about the poem's irony, meter and rhyme, on which see especially Sarah Stanbury Smith, "'Adam Lay I-Bowndyn' and the *Vinculum Amoris*," *English Language Notes* 15 (1977–8): 98–101; and Thomas G. Duncan, "The Text and Verse Form of 'Adam Lay I-Bowndyn,'" *Review of English Studies* NS 38 (1987): 215–21. I owe the emendation in line 7 to Duncan. The poem has been widely anthologized, and is discussed in Boklund-Lagopoulou, "*I have a yong suster*" (2002), Gray, *Themes and Images in the Medieval English Religious Lyric* (1972), Oliver, *Poems Without Names* (1970), Reiss, *The Art of the Middle English Lyric* (1972), and Woolf, *The English Religious Lyric in the Middle Ages* (1968), but what has really ensured its popularity, as it has with many a good song, is its mixture of bright lyrics, engaging and attractive melody, and surprise.

Adam lay i-bowndyn,
Bowndyn in a bond.
Fowre thowsand wynter,
Thowt he not to long.   *Thowt = thought*

And al was for an appil,
An appil that he tok,
As clerkes fyndyn wretyn,   *clerkes = clerks, students; wretyn = MS omission*
Wretyn in here book.

Ne hadde the appil take ben,
The appil taken ben,

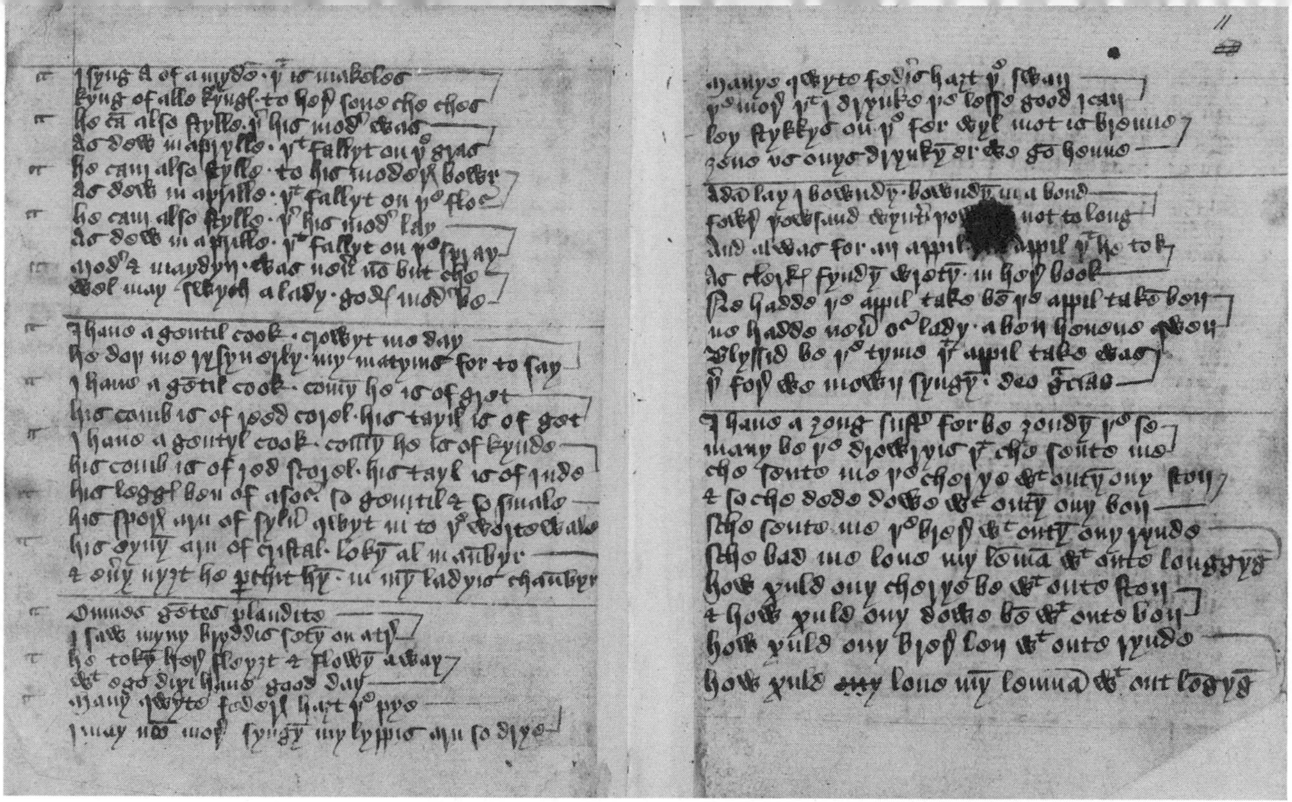

Figure 2 British Library Sloane MS 2593, folios 10v–11. This extraordinary collection of Middle English lyrics preserves some of the very best, and now most familiar, of the Middle English lyrics to have come down to us. It is associated with Bury St Edmunds, almost certainly with the great Benedictine abbey there, and the lyrics it contains were written in long lines, often with two lines run together, so as to save space. The folios shown here contain, among other texts, the sacred lyric "I syng of a mayden" (no. 13), followed immediately by the markedly secular lyric "I haue a gentil cok" (no. 39), and then by "Adam lay i-bowndyn" (no. 9), and these by "I haue a yong suster" (no. 33), which concludes on folio 11v. These are all unique texts, and without this manuscript they would not have been preserved.

Ne hadde neuer Our Lady
A ben heuene qwen!

Ne hadde neuer = never would . . . have

A = have

Blyssid be the tyme
That appil take was!
Therfore we mown syngyn
"Deo Gracias!"

mowen = may

trans. = Thanks be to God!

10

IMEV 2243. British Library, London. Harley MS 682, fol. 88v. Davies no. 90. Duncan B no. 7. Robbins no. 185. By Charles, Duke of Orleans.

Since the thirteenth century confession had been a widely practiced sacrament, one which laid emphasis on the responsibility of the individual Christian for his or her actions. Charles, Duke of Orleans, was taken prisoner at Agincourt in 1415, and spent the next 25 years an esteemed and noble prisoner in England. His clever and very courtly poem, which seems to have been written in English, not translated from French, turns on the witty construction that, according to the practices observed in the sacrament of confession, when something is stolen either it or its value must be returned to the person from whom it was taken before the priest can grant absolution. The voice and the intention are both playful here.

See two perceptive studies of Charles by A. C. Spearing, "Prison, Writing, Absence: Representing the Subject in the English Poems of Charles d'Orleans," *Modern Language Quarterly* 53 (1992): 83–99, and Enid McLeod, *Charles of Orleans, Prince and Poet* (New York: Viking Press, 1970).

My gostly fadir, Y me confesse, | *gostly fadir* = *spiritual confessor*
First to God and then to yow,
That at a window – wot ye how? – | *wot* = *know*
I stale a cosse of gret swetnes, | *stal a cosse* = *stole a kiss*
Which don was out avisynes, | *out avisynes* = *without deliberation*
But hit is doon, not vndoon, now.

My gostly fadir, Y me confesse,
First to God and then to yow,
But Y restore it shall, dowtles,
Ageyn, if so be that Y mow, | *mow* = *may*
And that to God Y make a vow, | *to* = MS omission
And ellis Y axe foryefnes. | *foryefnes* = *forgiveness*

My gostly fadir, Y me confesse,
First to God and then to yow.

11

IMEV 1866. Balliol College, Oxford. MS 354, fol. 223v. Davies no. 168.
Duncan B no. 126. Greene no. 11. Robbins no. 2.

This late medieval poem is a lively and attractive Christmas carol, one of many
which are discussed further in part X, below. It is here for its non-noble colle-
giality and for its warmth and good cheer. But it is worth remembering that,
as the courtesy books of the period indicate, a marshal in hall was in charge
of protocol and such a powerful man that Chaucer identifies the Host of the
Canterbury Tales as worthy to be "a marchal in an halle" (*General Prologue* 752).
At a Christmas feast he sometimes had the authority to send to the stocks
anyone who seemed not sufficiently merry, a fact which adds a certain edge to
the carol. The poem seems almost to resist the idea that Christmas is a religious
feast, though there may also be a note of conscious archaizing present, too.
It is cited from the commonplace book of Richard Hill, a London grocer and
merchant who inscribed the song about 1504. The refrain or burden comes
first, and is repeated (either by a leader or, more likely in this case, by the group)
after each stanza. As with other such songs, it gains more by performance before
a sympathetic group of the like-minded than by reading, though it gives a good
idea of what such songs and such celebration could involve.

   The very important manuscript which contains the poem, and the poem itself
are both discussed in Boklund-Lagopoulou, "*I have a yong suster*" (2002). MS Balliol
College 354 also contains no. 24 and no. 47, printed below, and is discussed in
the introduction, particularly note 16, above.

Make we mery, bothe more and lasse,
For now ys the tyme of Crystymas.

Lett no man cum into this hall,
Grome, page, nor yet marshall,   *yet marshall = even the marshall*
But that sum sport he bryng withall,   *sport = game, amusement*
For now ys the time of Crystmas.

Make we mery . . .

Yff that he say he can not syng,
Sum oder sport then lett hym bryng,
That yt may please at thys festyng,   *festyng = feast*
For now ys the time of Crystmas.

Make we mery . . .

Yff he say he can nowght do,
Then for my loue aske hym no mo,
But to the stokkes then lett hym go,
For now ys the tyme of Cristmas!

for my loue = for my sake
stokkes = stocks

Explicit.

Explicit = the end, it is finished

12

IMEV 4181. Brown C no. 119 (A, B, C).

Like other Middle English poems, this one exists in versions which differ one from another, but in this case the scribal (or poetic) intervention has been so marked as to constitute three separate versions. The lyric has been doubtfully attributed to Bishop Reginald Peacock who in the late 1450s was forced to recant certain of his theological opinions, but there is little support for this identification, which was probably made because Peacock was accused of insisting upon the fallibility of reason while urging the primacy of scripture – and thus by extension, of wonder. Since many late medieval religious lyrics were written by and for university students, who were and are expected to be amenable to reason, its championing of the spiritual, even ecstatic, quality of what was universally called "wonder" may have had special meaning for some among its first audience.

I have discussed the theological implications of one version of this lyric in "Fate, Faith and Paradox: Medieval Unlucky Days as a Context for 'Wytte Hath Wondyr,'" *Medium Aevum* 66 (1997): 288–92.

A British Library, London. Sloane MS 3534, fol. 3v

 Witte hath wondir that resoun ne telle kan,   *ne telle kan = cannot tell*
 How maidene is modir, and God is man,
 Leve thy resoun and bileve in the wondir,
 For feith is aboven and reson is vndir.

B Bodleian Library, Oxford. MS Lat. Liturg. E.10 (*SC* 32942), f. 22v

 Wytte hath wondyr that reson tell ne can,
 Houh a mayde bare a chylde both God and man.
 Therfore leve wytte and take to the wundyr,
 Feyth goth above, and reson goth vndyr.

C British Library, London. Harley MS 541, fol. 207v

 Wytte hath wonder how reson telle can,
 That mayd is mother and God is man,
 Oure noble sacrament, yn thre thinges on.
 In this leeve reson, beleve thou the wondre,
 There feith is lord, reson gothe vndre.

III

Poems Inscribed to the Blessed Virgin

In spite of the fact that her role in the gospels is really somewhat limited, poems directed toward, or written in praise of, the Blessed Virgin are among the most numerous of those inscribed in late medieval England. Many acknowledge her role as virgin and "Mother of God" (in Greek *Theotokos*, which earlier was the subject of controversy, but which became universally accepted after the Council of Chalcedon in 451), and record her role as a powerful intercessor on behalf of those who pray to her. Many, quite possibly most, such lyrics were written by men. Gender registers in these poems, but it is important not to credit the modern folk-belief that in the Middle Ages women were either universally worshiped or universally denigrated – or at least that these things happened far more often then than they do now. Probably the most important attribute of the Blessed Virgin was that she was human, chosen by God to be sure, but not herself a God, rather a human being, and, in the beginning at least, a human being like any other. She thus came to represent the very best that humankind could be, and the poems inscribed to her are, in a certain way, inscribed for all of humankind.

There is thus a powerful if latent Christian humanism present or implied in many of the poems directed to Mary or venerating what was universally understood to be her majesty. By honoring her, the poet honors all of humankind, himself or herself included. For many medieval poets, painters and theologians, the important moment in Mary's life was not the Nativity but the Annunciation – the very moment in which she agreed to become Christ's mother, so cooperating with the divine plan which was to lead to the salvation of humankind. Sometimes the poet will indicate to his or her reader that the word with which the angel greeted Mary at the time of the Annunciation, "Ave!" ("Hail!"), was the Latin name for Adam's partner, Eva, spelled backwards, and appropriately so, since Mary's role was to reverse, and so to set right, the "wrong" which Eve (and Adam!) had done in breaking God's command. Indeed, there was a very literal medieval belief that Mary actually conceived of Christ through her ear when she heard the angel speak, but no less important was the teaching that Mary had agreed to become God's mother – she had a choice, and happily for humankind she agreed to perform God's will. It was important to this tradition that she could have said no, and in many of these poems part of the surprise and delight which radiates out springs from the sense that human history could always have been otherwise, and would have been, had Mary demurred.

Studies of Mary and her role in the church are numerous, and for many questions the appropriate entry in the *Catholic Encyclopedia* will suffice. But for her role in the early church see Luigi Gambero, *Mary and the Fathers of the Church: The Blessed Virgin Mary in Patristic Thought*, trans. Thomas Buffer (San Francisco: Ignatius Press, 1999), and for its development, Mary F. Foskett, *A Virgin Conceived: Mary and Classical Representations of Virginity* (Bloomington and Indianapolis: Indiana University Press, 2002). There is a non-historical theological study by Ignace de la Potterie, SJ, *Mary in the Mystery of the Covenant*, trans. Bertrand Buby, SM (New York: Alba House, 1992), which contains, *inter alia*, a study of the Annunciation relevant to certain of the lyrics, pp. 3–35, and a perceptive study of the implication for the lyric by Thomas J. Heffernan, "The Virgin as an Aid to Salvation in Some Fifteenth-Century English and Latin Verses," *Medium Aevum* 52 (1983): 229–38.

13

IMEV 1367. British Library, London. Sloane MS 2593, fol. 10v. Brown C no. 81.
Davies no. 66. Duncan A no. 79. Gray no. 6.

Quite possibly the greatest of all Middle English lyrics, a sophisticated, allusive, and engaging poem, which is both simple yet complex, affecting yet detached, reflective yet celebratory. Just as poems about the Nativity often encode Christ's Passion, so this poem, so ostensibly about the Annunciation, encodes Christ's birth, which it identifies both in natural and scriptural imagery, and as a lover coming to his beloved. The poem, which seems to have been widely known in spite of being preserved in only one manuscript (see figure 2, p. 39), is focused upon the Annunciation, the very moment when Mary's acceptance of her role as Christ's mother meant that he came into her womb, and implicitly answers (without actually raising it) the very medieval question: How can a child be born of a Virgin? Its focus on the stillness of the moment of conception owes something to *Wisdom* 18.14 ("For while all things were in quiet silence, and the night in the midst of her course, Thy almighty word leapt down from heaven, from thy royal throne"), but even more to the silence which traditionally attends upon moments of supreme and sacred importance.

The dew which appears in the lyric has engaged much scholarly attention, and among other things figures throughout the Hebrew Scriptures as a symbol for renewal and joy (Hos. 14.6 "I will be as the dew," Is. 26.19 "for thy dew is the dew of the light," etc.). The natural and scriptural imagery in the poem is subtly but firmly drawn, and the scriptural references are particularly appropriate in a lyric which has been identified by Alan J. Fletcher as having been so well known that it was cited in Latin sermons ("'I Syng of a Maiden': A Fifteenth-Century Sermon Reminiscence," *Notes and Queries* 223 (1978): 107–8, 541). The feast of the Annunciation, so central to this lyric, was celebrated on March 25, at the beginning of spring.

The language and imagery of the poem have attracted much attention: among many studies, see in particular Barbara C. Raw, "'As Dew in April,'" *Modern Language Review* 55 (1960): 411–14; Michael Steffes, "'As Dewe in Aprylle': I Syng of a Mayden and the Liturgy," *Medium Aevum* 71 (2002): 63–73; and Virginia A. Moran, "The Meaning of 'Makeles' in 'I Syng of a Myden': A Dispute in Scholarship," *Nassau Review* 2 (1973): 24–8, which suggests a fourth meaning for the word, "peerless among all humans," a condition Moran links to the Immaculate Conception. An early critical study is Stephen Manning, "'I Syng of a Myden,'" *PMLA* 75 (1960): 8–12, later developed in his book, *Wisdom and Number* (1962), pp. 158–67; but see *contra* David G. Halliburton, "The Maden Makeles," *Papers on Language and Literature* 4 (1968): 115–20, which argues that Mary's uniqueness comes from her choice, not her lack of a partner. There are numerous later studies, and the poem has been treated in virtually all recent critical accounts of the Middle English lyric, see Boklund-Lagopoulou, *"I have a yong suster"* (2002), Gray, *Themes and Images in the Medieval English Religious Lyric* (1972) (particularly!), Oliver, *Poems Without Names* (1970), Reiss, *The Art of the Middle English Lyric* (1972), Sarah Appleton Weber, *Theology and Poetry in the Middle English Lyric: A Study of Sacred History and Aesthetic Form* (1969), and Woolf, *The English Religious Lyric in the Middle Ages* (1968).

I syng of a mayden
That is makeles.   *makeles* = a triple pun: *without equal, lover, or stain*
Kyng of alle Kynges,
To here sone she ches.   trans. = *she chooses for her son*

He cam also stylle,   *also stille* = *as silently*
Ther his moder was,
As dewe in Aprylle
That fallyt on the gras.

He cam also stylle
To his moderes bowr,   *bowr* = *bower, inner chamber, bedroom*
As dew in Aprille
That fallyt on the flour.

He cam also stylle
Ther his moder lay,   *lay* = *was*
As dew in Aprille
That fallyt on the spray.   *spray* = *a branch in flower*

Moder and maydyn
Was never non but che.   *che* = *she*
Wel may swych a lady   *swych* = *such*
Godes moder be!

14

IMEV 2645. British Library, London. Egerton MS 613, fol. 2 and Trinity College Cambridge MS 323, fol. 24v. Brown A no. 17A, 17B. Davies no. 5. Duncan A no. 75. Gray no. 7.

The evident warmth of this poem, both spiritual and personal, together with its fascination with, and eagerness to explore, some of Mary's many titles, make it a particularly attractive Marian lyric. Throughout, however, the poet also is subtly developing, in a lyrical voice, a theological argument which seeks to identify Mary's role as intercessor, Mother of God, and mediator between God and humankind. Indeed toward the end Mary almost becomes cooperative with her son in securing human salvation.

The order of stanzas followed here is that indicated by annotation in the manuscript and first noticed by Gray. On the very interesting manuscript in which it appears, see Betty Hill, "British Library MS Egerton 613," *Notes and Queries* 223 (1978): 394–409, 492–501. I have preferred certain readings from Egerton. The poem has been discussed in Stephen Manning, *Wisdom and Number: Toward a Critical Appraisal of the Middle English Religious Lyric* (1962) and Oliver, *Poems Without Names* (1970).

Of on that is so fayr and bright	*Of on that* = *of one who*
Velud maris stella,	trans. = as is the star of the sea
Brighter than the dayis light,	
Parens et puella	trans. = parent (mother) and maiden
Ic crie to thee, thou se to me,	*Ic* = *I; se* = *see*
Leuedy, preye thi sone for me,	*Leuedy* = *lady*
Tam pia,	trans. = so gracious
That Ic mote come to the,	*Ic mote* = *I may*
Maria.	
Leuedi, flour of alle thing,	*Leuedi* = *lady*
Rosa sine spina,	trans. = rose without thorn
Thou bere Ihesu, heuene king,	*bere* = *bore*
Gratia divina.	trans. = by divine grace
Of alle thou berst the pris	*pris* = *highest value, worth, prize*
Leuedi, Quene of Paradys	
Electa,	trans. = the chosen one
Mayde milde, moder	
Es effecta.	trans. = you are proven

Of kare conseil thou ert best, *kare conseil = in consolation; ert = are*
Felix fecundata. trans. = happy fruitfulness
Of alle wery thou ert rest,
Mater honorata. trans. = esteemed mother
Bisek him wit milde mod, *Bisek = ask; wit = with; mod = mood*
That for ous alle sad is blod, *ous = us; sad is = shed his*
In cruce. trans. = on the cross
That we moten komen til hym
In luce. trans. = in [heaven's] light

Al this world was forlore *forlore = forlorn, lost*
Eva peccatrice trans. = Eve having sinned
Tyl our lord was ybore *ybore = born*
De te geneitrice. trans. = from you, his mother
With "Ave" it went away,
Thuster nyht, and comth the day *Thuster = dark; comethe = came*
Salutis, trans. = of salvation
The welle springet hut of the *hut = out*
Virtutes. trans. = of virtues

Wel he wot he is thi sone *wot = knows*
Ventre quem portasti, trans. = whom you carried in womb
He wyl nout werne the thi bone, *werne = refuse; bone = request*
Parvum quem lactasti. trans. = whom you suckled when small
So hende and so god he his, *hende = wise; god = good; his = is*
He hauet brout ous to blis *hauet brout ous = has brought us*
Superni, trans. = on high
That haues hidut the foule pit, *haues hidut = has closed*
Inferni. trans. = of hell

Explicit cantus iste.

15

IMEV 1077. British Library, London. MS Arundel 285, fol. 196v–197. Brown C no. 21. Davies no. 179. Duncan B no. 49. Gray no. 62.

Written in the polished diction popular in late medieval Scottish poetry, this text also begins with some of Mary's many liturgically and scripturally based titles ("Queen of Heaven" and "Star of Bliss" were titles universally identified with Mary by the late medieval period), but plays on paradox and contradiction in the manner of seventeenth-century English metaphysical poetry, becoming finally a lyric of veneration and praise. But the direct address in the poem is not simply rhetorical. It also radiates a human warmth and even a kind of intellectual extravagance and curiosity along with its evidently felt and genuine veneration.

Haill, Quene of Hevin and Steren of Blis!   *Steren = star*
Sen that thi Sone thi Fader is,   *Sen that = since*
How suld he ony thing the warn,   *warn = refuse*
And thou his mothir, and he thi barn?   *barn = child*

Haill, Fresche Fontane that Springes New!
The rute and crope of all vertu,   *rute and crope = root and top*
Thou polist gem without offence,   *polist = polished; offence = flaw*
Thou bair the Lambe of Innocence.   *bair = bore, gave birth to*

Finis.

16

IMEV 1351. British Library, London. Sloane MS 2593, fol. 32–32v. Davies no. 77. Duncan A no. 80. Greene no. 143.

As much lullaby as carol (in fact it is both), this fifteenth-century song, powerfully recorded by the King's College Choir, Cambridge, in the late twentieth century, shows that late medieval mixture of veneration for Mary and adoration of Christ which sometimes seems almost to attest to an equality, but which usually (as here) remain separate. Christ is eternal (*eche*) and creator, Lord of lords and King of kings, but also a human infant, a dear darling, both God and Man. The angels sing and speak first of all to Christ, who is blessed, and then add that Mary is also, thus attesting to her subordination. The people, making Christmas joy, pray first to that child for his blessing, and then to his mother too.

Lullay, myn lykyng,   *lykyng = beloved*
my dere sone, myn swetyng,
Lullay, my dere herte,
myn owyn dere derlyng.

I saw a fayr mayden
Sytten and synge
Sche lullyd a lytyl chyld,
A swete lordyng.

Lullay, myn lykyng . . .

That eche Lord is that   *eche = eternal*
That made alle thinge,
Of alle lordis he is Lord,
Of alle kynges Kyng.

Lullay, myn lykyng . . .

Ther was mekyl melody   *mekyl = great*
At that chyldes berthe,
Alle tho wern in heuene blys,   *tho wern = those who were*
They made mekyl merth.

Lullay, myn lykyng . . .

"Aungele bryght," thei song that nyght,
And seydyn to that chyld,
"Blessid be thou, and so be sche
That is bothe mek and myld."   *myld = gracious*

Lullay, myn lykyng . . .

Prey we now to that chyld,
And to his moder dere,
Grawnt hem his blyssyng
That now makyn chere.   *makyn chere = are joyful, make joy*

Lullay, myn lykyng . . .

IV

Poems of Narrative Reflection

It is important to remember that, in the medieval period as in the modern, poems do not simply present states of being or of emotion, whether love, adoration, or apprehension. They rather give evidence of thought, indeed they are often inseparable from thought and reflection, and so can reveal the very process which brought them into being. Medieval lyrics, in English as in other languages, tend to be both scripturally and theologically allusive, and visually imagistic, and that is particularly true of the first poem printed here, which also reveals a thoughtful engagement of a world in which the poet is inescapably involved. Notice in particular the verbs in the poems which follow, and see the ways in which they act to determine meaning, and to assign (and curtail) significance.

But it is useful to remember that, even though they are intended to engage and to instruct the reader, these poems are explorations rather than demonstrations. They seek to encourage their reader to consider, not convert. In addition, the voice of the narrator must be taken seriously, and not read, or not always read, simply as surrogate for the poet. There are literary conventions present throughout (that of a dream vision, in which the persona of the narrator is led by his experiences in a dream to a higher truth than the one with which he fell asleep, is the most important), but these poems preserve a freshness and a power unusual in the period. And with their emphasis on Christ's Incarnation and Passion, meaning and significance are at their very heart.

Probably in the first and third of these poems, more than in any other in this anthology, you can see at work a uniquely English way of constructing narrative and philosophical reflection. Like other poems, but at greater length, these draw upon literary conventions which have their roots in biblical, philosophical, Latin and continental practice, but which are here pointedly empirical. It is not so much that there is a "literal level" to certain of these apparently symbolic conventions, as that their sense of actuality is as important as any other realities which they encode or defend. In reading these poems (as in others), it is important to remain alert to the sense that the narrative action and philosophical reflection which is being presented could always be otherwise. There is nothing necessarily "fated" about the physical or the philosophical outcomes which emerge, and the sense of surprise and wonder which they evoke is present in other good poems, medieval or not, and is integral to their meaning here.

17

IMEV 1463. Cambridge University Library. MS Hh.4.12, fol. 44v–47, with certain variants from MS Lambeth 853, pages 7–14 (the two MSS are fully collated in Gray). Duncan A no. 73. Gray no. 43.

This fifteenth-century poem opens with Christ represented as sitting (a traditional pose of literary complaint), lamenting his treatment at the hands of the one he loves. The poet has formed his lyric by combining brilliantly an extraordinary number of traditional devotions and dramatic conventions – thus Christ uses the liturgical "Reproaches" associated with the Good Friday liturgy, and assumes the pose of the Lover-Knight, ready to die for the love of his Lady (usually identified with the church), who following the tradition of the arming of the knight, buckles him into his armor, but then takes refuge in the wound in his side, which has now (in yet another alteration) become her chamber, where she can wash herself (by implication in Christ's saving blood), though Christ also sits like a lover awaiting his beloved so that they may withdraw into the enclosed garden of Paradise and of the Psalms. Indeed, at one point Christ changes gender, and becomes himself a mother (the image occurs elsewhere in medieval devotional literature, including chapter 60 of Julian of Norwich's *Revelations*) so as to suckle his infant church, and through her, all persons. Throughout this remarkable poem, Christ has been the lover, spouse, brother, mother, and finally husband to all of humankind.

On Christ as a Lover-Knight in these lyrics (and elsewhere) see Rosemary Woolf, "The Theme of Christ the Lover Knight in Medieval English Literature," *Review of English Studies* 13 (1962): 1–16. The poem has been the object of important studies by Thomas D. Hill, "Androgyny and Conversion in the Middle English Lyric, 'In the vaile of restles mynd,'" *ELH* 53 (1986): 459–70, and Mary-Ann Stouck, "'In a valey of this restles mynde': Contexts and Meaning," *Modern Philology* 85 (1987–8): 1–11. Douglas Gray has pointed out some important typological allusions in the poem in "Typology in Some Medieval English Religious Lyrics," in Hugh T. Keenan, ed., *Typology and English Medieval Literature* (New York: AMS Press, 1992), pp. 275–88, especially pp. 278–9.

In the vaile of restles mynd	*vaile* = vale, valley
I sowght in mownteyn and in mede,	*mede* = meadow
Trustyng a treu lofe for to fynd.	*treu lofe* = true love
Vpon an hyll than toke I hede,	
A voise I herd, and nere I yede,	*yede* = went
In gret dolour complaynyng tho –	*dolour* = sorrow; *tho* = then
"See, dere Soule, my sydes blede,	*blede* = bleed
Quia amore langueo."	trans. = because I languish in love

Vpon thys mownt I fand a tree,   *mownt = mount, mountain; fand = found*
Vndir thys tree a man sittyng.
From hede to fote wowndyd was he,
Hys herte blode I saw bledyng,
A semely man to be a kyng,   *semely = attractive*
A graciose face to loke vnto.
I asked him how he had paynyng,   *had paynyng = had (come to have) pain*
He said, "*Quia amore langueo.*"

"I am treu love that fals was neuer,
My sister, mannys soule, I loved hyr thus,
Bycause I wold on no wyse disseuere   *disseuere = separate*
I left my kyngdome gloriouse.
I purueyd hyr a paleis preciouse. *purueyd = provided; paleis = palace* (Lambeth)
She flytt, I folowyd, I luffed her soo   *luffed = loved*
That I suffred thes paynes piteuouse,   *piteuouse = pitiable*
Quia amore langueo.

"My faire love and my spouse bryght,
I saved hyr fro betyng, and she hath me bett,   *bett = beaten*
I clothed hyr in grace and heuenly lyght,
This blody surcote she hath on me sett.   *surcote = scherte* (Lambeth)
For langyng love I will not lett.   *lett = cease*
Swete strokys ben thes, Loo!
I haf loved euer als I hett,   *als I hett = as I promised*
Quia amore langueo.

"I crownyd hyr with blysse, and she me with thorne,
I led hyr to chambre, and she me to dye,
I browght hyr to worship, and she me to skorne,   *worship = honor*
I dyd hir reuerence, and she me velanye.   *velanye = villainy, shame*
To love, that loveth is no maistrye,   *trans. = to love [he] who loves you is no skill*
Hyr hate made never my love hyr foo,   *foo = foe*
Ask than no moo questions whye,
But *quia amore langueo.*

"Loke vnto myn handys, Man.
Thes gloues were geuen me whan I hyr sowght.   *gloues = gauntlets?*
They be nat white, but rede and wan,   *wan = discolored*
Embrodred with blode – my spouse hem browght.

They wyll not of, I leve hem nowght.   *of = off*
I wowe hyr with them where evere she goo,
Thes handes full frendly for hyr fowghte,
Quia amore langueo.

"Maruell not, Man, thof I sitt styll.   *thof = though*
My love hath shod me wondyr strayte.
She boklyd my fete, as was hyr wyll,   *fete = feet*
With sharp nailes, wel thow maist waite,   *waite = see*
In my love was neuer dissaite,   *dissaite = deceit*
For all my membres I haf opynd hyr to,   *membres = limbs*
My body I made hyr hertys baite,   *hyr . . . baite = bait for her heart*
Quia amore langueo.

"In my syde I haf made hyr nest,
Loke in me, how wyde a wound is here.
This is hyr chambre, here shal she rest,
That she and I may slepe in fere.   *in fere = together*
Here may she wasshe, if any filth were,
Here is socour for al hyr woo.
Cum if she will, she shall haf chere,   *chere = good company*
Quia amore langueo.

"I will abide till she be redy.
I will hir sue if she say nay.   *hir sue* (Lambeth) = MS *to her send* or
If she be rechelesse I will be redy.   *rechelesse = negligent; redy = attentive*
If she be dawngerouse, I will hyr preye.   *dawngerouse = disdainful*
If she do wepe, than byd I nay.
Myn armes ben spred to clypp hyr to,   *clypp = embrace*
Crye onys 'I com,' now, Sowle, assaye,   *onys = once; assaye = try*
Quia amore langueo.

"I sitt on an hille for to se farre.   *se farre = see far*
I loke to the vayle, my spouse I see.
Now rynne she awayward, now cummyth she narre,   *narre = near*
Yet fro myn eyesight she may not be.
Sum waite ther pray, to make hyr flee,   *waite = lie in wait for*
I rynne tofore to chastise hyr foo.   *tofore = ahead*
Recouer, my Soule, agayne to me,   *Recouer = return*
Quia amore langueo.

"My swete spouse, let us go   *let us go playe* (Lambeth) = MS *will we goo play?*
   playe.
Apples ben rype in my gardine,   *ben rype* = *are ripe*
I shall clothe the in new array,
Thy mete shall be mylk, honye, and wyne,
Now, dere Soule, latt us go dyne,
Thy sustenaunce is in my   *skryppe* = *pouch, satchel* (Lambeth) = MS *cryppe*
   skryppe, Loo!
Tary not now, fayre spouse myne,
Quia amore langueo.

"Yf thow be fowle, I shall thee make clene,   *thee* (Lambeth) = MS omission
Yf thou be seke, I shall the hele,   *seke* = *sick*
Yf thou owght morne, I shal   *owght morne* = *anything desire; bemene* = *comfort*
   bemene,
Spouse, why will thow nowght with me dele?
Thou fowndyst never love so lele,   *lele* = *faithful*
What wilt thow, Soule, that I shal do?
I may of vnkyndnes the appele,   *vnkyndnes* = *ingratitude; appele* = *accuse*
Quia amore langueo.

"What shall I do now with my spouse?
Abyde I will hyr iantilnesse.   *iantilnesse* = *gentility, nobility*
Wold she loke onys owt of hyr howse
Of flesshely affecciouns and vnclennesse.
Hyr bed is made, hyr bolstar is in blysse,
Hyr chambre is chosen, suche ar no moo!
Loke owt at the wyndows of kyndnesse,
Quia amore langueo.

"Long and love thou neuer   trans. = *though you love long and intensively;*
   so hygh,   this stanza follows the next one in Lambeth
Yit is my love more than thyn may be,
Thow gladdyst, thow wepist,   *gladdyst* = *rejoice; by* = MS *bygh* = *beside*
   I sitt the by.
Yet myght thow, Spouse, loke onys at me!
Spouse, shuld I alway fede the
With childys mete? Nay, Love, nat so!
I preve thi love with adversite,   *preve thi* (Lambeth) = *test thy*
Quia amore langueo.

"My spouse is in hir chambre – hald
   yowr pease,
Make no noyse, but lat hyr slepe,
My babe shal sofre noo disease.
I may not here my dere childe wepe
For with my pappe I shal hyr kepe.
No wondyr thowgh I tend hyr to,
Thys hoole in my side had neuer ben so depe,
But *quia amore langueo*.

"Wax not wery, myn owne dere wyfe!
What mede is aye to lyffe in counfort?
For in tribulacioun I ryn more ryfe,
Ofter tymes than in disport.
In welth, in woo, euer I support.
Than, dere Soule, go neuer me fro,
Thy mede is markyd, whan thow art mort
In blisse – *quia amore langueo*."

hir (Lambeth) = MS omission

lat = let
sofre = suffer

pappe = teat

Wax = grow
mede = reward; *aye* = ever; *lyffe* = live
ryn = run; *ryfe* = quickly
disport = pleasure

mort = dead

18

IMEV 139. Cambridge University Library. MS Ff. 1.6, fol. 137v–138. Robbins no. 167.

Almost certainly written by a woman, possibly by one Margery Hungerford, one of four women whose names appear in the fifteenth-century manuscript which contains this lyric and others. This felt and engaging lyric is more secular meditation than conventional love-lyric. It is found in the Findern Anthology, a collection of lyrics which include several by women, and whose importance is only now becoming understood. There is an introduction at the beginning of Appendix C, below, which contains three additional poems from this extraordinary manuscript, together with a short discussion of the manuscript itself and its contents.

The language of this love-lyric is both simple and affecting, and either in spite of or because of its conventional narrative setting it advances with a certain emotional power. The shift of the spelling of the first person singular pronoun from "Y" to "I" which occurs within the lyric is scribal.

Alas, alas, and alas, why
Hath Fortune done so crewelly,
Fro me to take away the seyte   *seyte* = *sight*
Of that that gewrt my hert lyte?   *gewrt* = *causes; lyte* = *to be lightened*

Of all thyng that in erth Y se,
To me hyt was the most blyse
Whan that Y was in thy presense   *thy* = *MS omission*
To wham my hert doth reuerense.

And euer schal, for well or woo,
Or drede of frende, or lyf allsoo,   *allsoo* = *also*
Hit schal me neuer other asterte,   *asterte* = *escape*
But ye to haue my hole hert.

Saue whan I come to the deth,
That nedes oute mouste the brethe,
That kepyth the lyfe me withinne,
And than fro yow most I twyne.   *twyne* = *part*

And tyl the day hit me owre,   trans. = *and until the day it (death) overcomes me*
Ryght feythfully I yow ensure,

That ther schal no erthly thyng   *erthly* = MS *erly*
On my part make departyng.

Thus ame I sett yn stable wyse   *ame* = *am*
To lefe and dure in yowre seruyce,   *lefe and dure* = *live and endure*
Wytoute faynyng of my hert
Thow I fele neuer soo grete smert.

19

IMEV 1402. Bodleian Library, Oxford. MS Eng. poet. a.1, "The Vernon Manuscript" (*SC* 3938–42), now kept as MS Arch F.a.1., fol. 409 col. 3–409v col. 1. Brown B no. 106. Davies no. 48. Duncan A no. 61. Gray no. 83.

This simply extraordinary fourteenth-century poem engages directly, as relatively few Middle English lyrics do, the issue of religious doubt, and in particular as it confronts the problem of evil. It draws some of its language, imagery, and thought from the first chapter of Ecclesiastes, in particular its images concerning the apparent purposelessness of the daily movement of the sun from east to west; of the flowing of rivers into a sea which is never any more full because of them; of the passing of generation after generation; and of the apparently random and perhaps meaningless death of man and beast alike. The poem uses these images and other literary devices to raise the most important of questions: Since there is a good and powerful God, why is the world as we see it? Is the death of a person really any different from that of an animal, and if so in what way? Is any one sect, or school of theology, really better than another? And above all, how do I know what I know? And do I have a purpose?

In a pioneering article, Dom Gerard Sitwell referred to this poem's "apparent agnosticism," which he thought tempered by an evident acknowledgment of God's existence, and suggested that the poem really concerns itself with God's foreknowledge, an issue raised in *De Causa Dei*, the 1344 work of Thomas of Bradwardine, sometime fellow of Merton College, Oxford, and briefly Archbishop of Canterbury. But although knowing is an important theme in the poem (the poem begins ironically by asking knowledge of "some wise man," and words like "witen," "wot," "thenk," "kenne," "resoun," "hou and why," and "know" run like a leitmotif throughout), the issue is not so much *what* God knows, as the nature of divine knowledge itself, and the difficulties, even when reflecting upon the apparently random meaninglessness of creation, of comparing what human beings know to what God does. The sense here is that it is our fate and our condition to see in a glass darkly (though *that* Pauline text is not cited!), and that the apparently immortal earth on which we reside, the theological and other books on which we rely, are finally nothing, are only a construction and a fantasy, so that we should rather make merry and banish care, knowing that the only verities with which we must contend are our life, our conscience, and our God, and that our end is ever hopeful.

See further Dom Gerard Sitwell, OSB, "A Fourteenth-Century English Poem on Ecclesiastes," *Dominican Studies* 3 (1950): 285–90. The late fourteenth-century manuscript from which I have edited the poem has been named for Col. Edward Vernon, its seventeenth-century donor to the Bodleian Library, Oxford, and is one of the largest and heaviest manuscripts of vernacular poetry (most of it religious, in this case) to have come down to us from late medieval England.

It now contains 350 of what were originally 422 (or 426) folios, each measuring $22\frac{1}{2}$ by $15\frac{1}{2}$ inches (544 × 393 mm); the whole now weighs over 48 pounds, but it would, when complete, have weighed over 50. Difficult to handle, difficult in which to locate a particular text, even difficult (because of its size) to read, the expense of causing such a manuscript to be written suggests a noble owner, though Vernon has too a less complete sister manuscript now in the British Library, London, Additional MS 22283, called the Simeon manuscript after an early owner. (Bracketed readings below are present in Simeon.) Both manuscripts in fact contain a large number of religious and moral texts, including the present poem, Douglas Gray's edition of which is based on Simeon. See further Derek Pearsall, ed., *Studies in the Vernon Manuscript* (Cambridge: D. S. Brewer, 1990), *passim*, and especially A. I. Doyle, "The Shaping of the Vernon and Simeon Manuscripts," pp. 1–13. There is a huge facsimile of the Vernon manuscript (which is still only 92 percent of the original manuscript in size) edited and with an introduction by A. I. Doyle, *The Vernon Manuscript: A Facsimile of Bodleian Library, Oxford, MS Eng. Poet. A.1* (Cambridge: D. S. Brewer, 1987).

I point out that some editions reasonably change what is in the manuscripts, placing the last stanza as coming fifth in order, so as to provide a more conventional (or perhaps more fitting) conclusion, and that keeping the order which is in the manuscripts (as I have here) has the effect of ending the poem with a stark reminder that everything in the world, the biggest of trees, "man, horse and hound" all pass away, so that everything goes "from nought to nought." The scribal error, if that is what it was, concludes the poem with a (too modern?) reference (to the tree) which offers an image of failed power and uncertainty to the ending. The order in the manuscripts thus presents their reader with a differing, and unsettling effect, even though it may not be what the author intended. But if you were editing this poem, would you move the stanza?

I wolde witen of sum wys wiht,	trans. = *I would know from some wise person*
Witerly, what this world were.	*Witerly* = *truly*
Hit fareth as a foules fliht,	*fareth . . . fliht* = *goes like bird's flight*
Now is hit henne, now is hit here,	*henne* = *far away*
Ne be we neuer so muche of miht,	*miht* = *strength*
Now be we on benche, nou be we on bere,	*bere* = *bier (i.e. dead)*
And be we neuer so war and wiht,	*war and wiht* = *aware and strong*
Now be we sek, now beo we fere,	*sek* = *sick; fere* = *healthy*
Now is on proud, withouten peere,	*peere* = *peer, equal*
Now is the selue I set not by,	*selue . . . by* = *one of whom I thought nothing*
And whos wol alle thing her[t]ly here,	trans. = *whoever will willingly hear all*
This world fareth as a fantasy.	

The sonnes cours we may wel kenne,   *kenne = see, know*
Aryseth Est and geth doun West.
The ryuers into the see thei renne,   *see = sea*
And hit is neuer the more almest,   *almest = hardly*
Wyndes rosshen her and henne,   *rosshen = rush; her and henne = here and there*
In snough and reyn is non arest.   *snough = snow; arest = stopping*
Whon this wol stunte, ho wot or   *Whon = when; stunte = stop;*
    whenne,   *ho wot = who knows*
But only God on grounde grest?   *on grounde grest = greatest on earth*
The eorthe in on is euer prest,   *trans. = the earth is ever the same*
Now bidropped, now al druyghe,   *bidropped = wet with dew; druyghe = dry*
But vche gome glit forth as a   *trans. = each man leaves as (if he were only)*
    gest.   *a guest*
This world fareth as a fantasye.

Kunredes come, and kunredes gon,   *Kunredes = kindred, ancestors; gon = go*
As ioynen generacions.   *ioynen = MS ioyneth = join*
But alle heo passeth, euerchon,   *euerchon = everyone*
For al heor preparacions,
Sum are forgete clene as bon,   *forgete = forgotten; bon = bone*
Among alle maner nacions.   *maner nacions = kinds of nations*
So schul men thenken vs   *thenken vs nothing on = think nothing of us*
    nothing on,
That nou han the ocupacions.   *trans. = that have (our former) occupations*
And alle theos disputacions
Idelyche all vs ocupye   *Idelyche = in vain*
For Crist maketh the creacions,
And this world fareth as a fantasye.

Which is Mon, ho wot and what,   *Which = what kind of thing*
Whether that he be ought or nouht?
Of erthe and eyr groweth vp a gnat,   *eyr = air; a gnat = a gnat (a bug)*
And so doth mon whon al is souht.   *is = MS his; souht = examined*
Thaugh mon be waxen gret and fat,   *waxen = grown*
Mon melteth awey so deth a mouht.   *so . . . mouht = as does a moth*
Monnes miht nis worth a mat,   *mat = a mat (a worthless object)*
But nuygheth himself and turneth   *nuygheth = vexes; nought = nothing*
    to nought.
Ho wot, saue He that al hath wrought,
Wher mon bicometh whon he schal dye?

Ho knoweth bi dede, ought bote
  bi thought   trans. = *who knows about*
For this world fareth as a fantasye.   *death except by thought*

Dyeth mon, and beestes dye,
And al is on occasion.   trans. = *and it's all the same* (lit.: *one happening*)
And alle o deth bos bothe drye,   trans. = *and but one death these both shall suffer*
And han on incarnacion.   *on incarnacion* = *one birth, the same beginning*
Saue that men beoth more slyghe,   *slyghe* = *intelligent*
Al is o comparison.   *o comparison* = *alike*
Ho wot, yif monnes soule styghe,   *styghe* = *rises*
And bestes soule synketh doun?
Who knoweth beestes entencioun,
On heor creatour how thei crie,
Saue only God that knoweth heore soun?   *soun* = *language*
For this world fareth as a fantasye.

Vche secte hopeth to be saue,   *secte* = *(religious) group, sect; saue* = *saved*
Baldely, bi heore bileeue.   trans. = *boldly, because of their teachings*
And vchon vppon God heo craue.   *craue* = *cry*
Whi schulde God with hem him greue?   *greue* = *take trouble*
Vchon trouweth that othur raue,   *trouweth* = *thinks; raue* = *are mad*
But alle heo cheoseth God for cheue,   trans. = *but all choose God as (their) chief*
And hope in God vchone thei haue,
And bi heore wit heore worching   *heore worching preue* = *their*
  preue.   *practices justify*
Thus mony maters men dou meue,   *meue* = *move, discuss*
Sechen heor wittes hou and why,   *Sechen* = *search*
But Godes merci vs alle biheue,   *biheue* = *is necessary for*
For this world fareth as a fantasy.

For thus men stumble and sere heore wittes,   *sere* = *burn, destroy*
And meueth maters mony and fele.   *fele* = *cruel*
Summe leeueth on him, sum leueth on hit,   *leeueth* = *believes; hit* = *that*
As children leorneth for to spel.
But non seoth non that   *seoth* = *says; abit* = *abides (no one says that*
  abit,   *anyone remains)*
Whon stilly deth wol on hym stele.   *stilly* = *silent; stele* = *steal*
For He that hext in heuene sit,   *hext* = *highest*
He is the help and hope of hele.   *hele* = *healing, salvation*

For wo is ende of worldes wele,   *wele = goods*
Vche lyf loke wher that I lye.   trans. = *let each one ask if I lie*
This world is fals, fikel and frele,   *frele = frail*
And fereth but as a fantasye.

Wharto wilne we for te knowe   trans. = *for what purpose do we seek to know*
The poyntes of Godes priuete?   *poyntes = points, details*
More then him lust us   trans. = *more than it pleases him to show; us* (Simeon)
    for te schowe,
We shulde not knowe in no degre,
An idel bost is for te blowe   *te blowe = to brag*
A Mayster of Diuinite!   trans. = *(like) a Master of Divinity*
Thenk we lyue in eorthe her lowe,   *Thenk = remember; lowe = below*
And God an heigh in mageste.
Of material mortualite   trans. = *of material mortality*
Medle we, and of no more maistrie.   *maistrie = understanding*
The more we trace the Trinite,   *trace = examine*
The more we falle in fantasye.

But leue we vre disputisoun,   *leue we = let us end*
And leeue on him that al hath wrought.   *leeue = trust*
We mowe no[t] preue bi no resoun   *preue = prove; no = any*
Hou he was born that al vs bought.
But hol in vre entencioun   *hol = whole; entencioun = intention*
Worschipe we him in hert and thought.
For he may turne kuyndes   *kuyndes = natures;*
    vpsedoun,   *vpsedoun = upside down*
That all kuyndes made of nought.
Whon al vr bokes ben forth bouht,   *vr bokes = our books; bouht = brought*
And al vr craft of clergye,   *craft = learning*
And al vr wittes ben thorwout sought,
Yit we fareth as a fantasye.

Of fantasye is al vr fare,   *fare = actions, doing*
Olde and yonge and all i-fare.   *i-fare = together*
But make we murie and sle care,   *sle = slay*
And worschipe we God, whil we ben here.
Spende vr good and luytel spare.
And vche mon cheries otheres cheere,   *cheries = encourages; cheere = happiness*
Thenk hou we comen hider al bare,
Vr wey wendyng is in a were.   *wendyng = of going; were = doubt*

Prey the Prince that hath no pere,   *pere = equal*
Tac vs hol to his merci,   *Tac = take; hol = wholly*
And kepe vr conscience clere,
For this world is but a fantasy.

[Bi ensaumple men may se
A gret treo groweth out of the grounde,
Nothing abated the eorthe wol be,   *abated = less, reduced*
Thaugh hit be huge, gret and rounde.
Riht ther wol rooten the selue tre,   *rooten = rot; selue = same*
Whon elde hath maad his kuynde   *elde = age; kuynde = nature;*
    aswounde,   *aswounde = weak*
Thaugh ther weore rote suche thre,   *trans. = though three such trees rotted*
The eorthe wol nat encrece a pounde.   *encrece = increase*
Thus waxeth and wanteth mon, hors and hounde,
From nought to nought thus henne we highe,   *henne we highe = hence we go*
And her we stunteth but a stounde,   *stunteth = remain; stounde = moment*
For this world is but a fantasye.]

V

Poems Whose Meanings Are Hidden (but Not Necessarily Unknown)

Sometimes one of the hardest questions to answer about a Middle English lyric has less to do with its meaning than with its form or use. Even when the language and sentiment are conventional, or at least seem to be so, it can be difficult to know what else is present, and why. On the other hand, there are lyrics which seem to resist interpretation less because they are concerned with Christian mysteries like the Trinity or mystical awareness, than because they allude to events which their contemporaries would have recognized at once, but which are now a closed book to most readers.

Changes having been made, this is a circumstance present in much modern poetry too. The American poet Wallace Stevens (1879–1955) brought his readers to an understanding of the mysteries he was revealing by a process of often exotic and even obscure images, not unlike the sort which occur in certain of the lyrics printed in this section. One of Stevens' most brilliant images appears in his poem "The Emperor of Ice Cream," but his emperor is actually that most medieval of personifications, Death, and the strangeness and unfamiliarity of an invented convention – which gains in meaning if we do *not* either forget or simply "translate" the image itself – lends power and authority to the poem. In another Stevens poem, "Anecdote of the Jar," the narrator places a meaningless blue bottle down in the Tennessee countryside, so that the apparently random lines of the countryside take on meaning by virtue of their relationship to it. A writer of medieval religious lyrics would have understood. But there are evident differences between medieval and modern images, as well. For one thing, modern imagistic patterns (and particularly those of Stevens!) were not constrained by biblical, devotional, or more broadly religious traditions, as medieval ones usually are. For another, the role of the artist is understood in different terms – but not, perhaps, in entirely different terms.

Thus, even when a lyric can be associated with a practice like the dance, its diction and meaning can remain a challenge even for a most perceptive reader. And yet, as with many modern poems, the "point" of these poems is not so much to reduce them to "meaning," as to understand how, in their undecoded form, that meaning may be communicated and grasped. Like many good poems, certain of the texts printed here can be understood even before their meaning is apparent, and their form, diction, and images are crucial to understanding what that meaning finally may be.

On Stevens see Helen Vendler, *Wallace Stevens: Words Chosen out of Desire* (Cambridge, Mass.: Harvard University Press, 1984, rpt. 1996), pp. 45–6 ("Anecdote of the Jar") and 50–3 ("The Emperor of Ice Cream").

20

IMEV 3891; *Supplement* 2037.5. Bodleian Library, Oxford. MS Rawlinson D. 913 (*SC* 13679), fol. 1v (h). Davies no. 33. Duncan A no. 118. Robbins no. 18.

One of the most haunting and finally mysterious lyrics to have come down from the medieval period, this poem may well have been or begun as a dance song, but it equally seems to have been sung in church, perhaps in a version differing from the one preserved, but still secular enough to shock some clerics. Thus we really do not know whether the song was sacred or secular, or depending upon the version or the circumstances, either or both. Did a secular lyric which seemed to incorporate religious language and imagery recommend itself to parish priests and others seeking a song the congregation would enjoy singing – and perhaps knew? Was a popular song sometimes at least partly reconfigured so as to provide for church usage, in this case by linking it to the Latin poem *Peperit virgo* whose line structure it can be made to follow, but then rejected by orthodoxy as too irredeemably secular to serve such a sacred purpose? Or did the sense of the fantastic, which the lyric so clearly encodes, suggest that a sacred significance must lie beneath its surface?

For two sharply contrasting accounts of this extraordinary poem see: D. W. Robertson, Jr., "Historical Criticism," in *English Institute Essays, 1950* (New York: Columbia University Press, 1951), pp. 3–31 (see especially p. 27), which reads the maiden in the poem as the Blessed Virgin, the cold water as God's grace, the violets as humility, the wilderness as the Old Law, etc.; Joseph Harris, "'Maiden in the Mor' and the Medieval Magdalene Tradition," *Journal of Medieval and Renaissance Studies* 1 (1971): 59–87, which argues for a religious reading of the lyric against the conversion and penance of Mary Magdalene; and Ronald Waldron, who reads the poem against the formulations employed in singing-games for children, ones which encode actual death, in "'Maiden In The Mor Lay' and the Religious Imagination," in Helen Philips, ed., *Langland, the Mystics and the Medieval English Religious Tradition: Essays in Honour of S. S. Hussey* (Cambridge: D. S. Brewer, 1990), pp. 215–22.

Against these (very different) religious interpretations, see the historical and secular readings: Richard L. Greene, "The Maid of the Moor in the *Red Book of Ossory*," *Speculum* 27 (1952): 504–6, and Siegfried Wenzel, "The Moor Maiden – A Contemporary View," *Speculum* 49 (1974): 69–74, which identifies contemporary ecclesiastical objections to the song being sung in church. It has also been examined as a probably secular dance song, which has features in common with the other poems with which it is associated in the manuscript record, in John Burrow's article "Poems without Context: The Rawlinson Lyrics," *Essays in Criticism* 29 (1979): 6–32, reprinted in Burrow's *Essays on Medieval Literature* (Oxford: Clarendon Press, 1984), pp. 1–26. For a more heavily edited version and a study of its manuscript and meter, see Thomas G. Duncan, "The Maid in the Moor and the Rawlinson Text," *Review of English Studies* NS 47 (1996): 151–62, which proposes a series of expansions, emendations and *Peperit virgo*-like line divisions which differ from those followed here. See further, nos 22 and 38 below, both also from the single strip of vellum now bound into the front of Bodleian Library, Oxford, MS Rawlinson D 913, which contains this and other lyrics (see figure 3, p. 75). The poem is further discussed in Boklund-Lagopoulou, *"I have a yong suster"* (2002), Oliver, *Poems Without Names* (1970), and Reiss, *The Art of the Middle English Lyric* (1972).

Maiden in the mor lay,	*mor = moor*
In the mor lay,	
Seuen nyst fulle,	*Seuen nyst = MS Seuenyst*
Seven nist fulle,	*nyst, nist, nistes = nights*
Maiden in the mor lay,	
In the mor lay,	
Seven nistes fulle	
Ant a day.	*Ant = and*
Welle wa[s] hire mete.	*wa[s] = MS wat; mete = food*
Wat was hire mete?	*Wat = what*
The primerole ant the,	*primerole = primrose*
The primerole ant the,	
Welle was hire mete.	
Wat was hire mete?	
The primerole	
Ant the violet.	
Welle was hire dryng,	*dryng = drink*
Wat was hire dryng?	
The chelde water of the,	*chelde = cold*
The chelde water of the,	
Welle was hire dryng,	
Wat was hire dryng?	
The chelde water	
Of the welle-spring.	
Welle was hire bour,	*bour = bedroom, inner chamber*
Wat was hire bour?	
The red rose an te,	*an te = and the*
The red rose an te,	

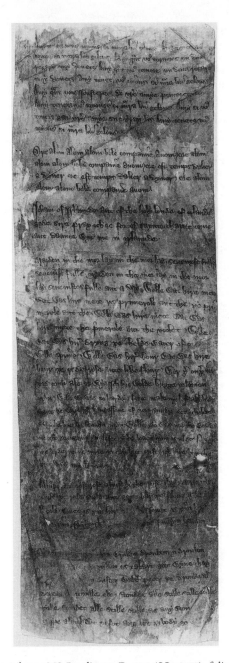

Figure 3 Bodleian Library MS Rawlinson D. 913 (*SC* 13679), folio 1v. Quite possibly the most valuable and important manuscript fragment in all of English literature, this leaf still contains, in a small, heavily abbreviated hand, the only known texts for "Maiden in the Mor Lay" (no. 20), "Ich Am of Irlaunde" (no. 22), and "Al Nist by the rose, Rose" (no. 38), among other poems. Although bound into the beginning of the Rawlinson manuscript, the fragment has no connection with any other item therein, and is not even whole in itself, having been cut down from a larger folio sometime in the past, but saving the texts it uniquely preserves.

Welle was hire bour,
Wat was hire bour?
The red rose
An te lilie flour.

21

IMEV 864. Bodleian Library, Oxford. MS Douce 139 (*SC* 21713), fol. 5. Brown A
no. 8. Davies no. 4. Duncan A no. 16.

This short but engaging lyric of about 1270 exists as a two-part song, and is accompanied by music in the manuscripts (see figure 4, p. 78). Here, as in other lyrics, the creatures which are described in nature – birds, fish, beasts – contrast with the speaker's "sorw," and the opposition seems to intensify his suffering. The "best of bone and blood" refers almost certainly to a secular beloved, who has rejected him, and thus provided the occasion for his lyric. As G. V. Smithers has pointed out in *Early Middle English Verse and Prose* (edited with J. A. W. Bennett, Oxford: Clarendon Press, 1966), p. 319, the phrase also appears in one of the Harley lyrics, *IMEV* 2207, line 5, and may be conventional, though it has also been taken as a reference to Christ, a construction which was not at all usual in these terms in Middle English verse of this period. The song has further been identified as a *reverdie*, a song welcoming spring, in which the lover contrasts his grieving for his lost love with the joys of the natural world around him, and the happiness of all other creatures.

The song performs well, and partly for that reason has provoked much criticism. See among other studies, Howell D. Chickering, Jr., "'Foweles in the Frith': A Religious Art-Song," *Philological Quarterly* 50 (1971): 115–20; Thomas C. Moser, Jr., "'And I Mon Waxe Wod': the Middle English 'Foweles in the Frith,'" *PMLA* 102 (1987): 326–37; and Richard H. Osberg, "Collocation and Theme in the Middle English Lyric 'Foweles in the Frith,'" *Modern Language Quarterly* 46 (1985): 115–27. It is further discussed in Oliver, *Poems Without Names* (1970) and Reiss, *The Art of the Middle English Lyric* (1972). But it has too a strangely enigmatic quality about it, one which continues to attract and engage readers and musicians alike.

Foweles in the frith,	*Foweles = birds; frith = woods*
The fisses in the flod,	*fisses = fishes; flod = sea*
And I mon waxe wod.	*mon = must; waxe wod = go mad*
Mulch sorw I walke with	
For beste of bon and blod.	*beste = best; bon = bone*

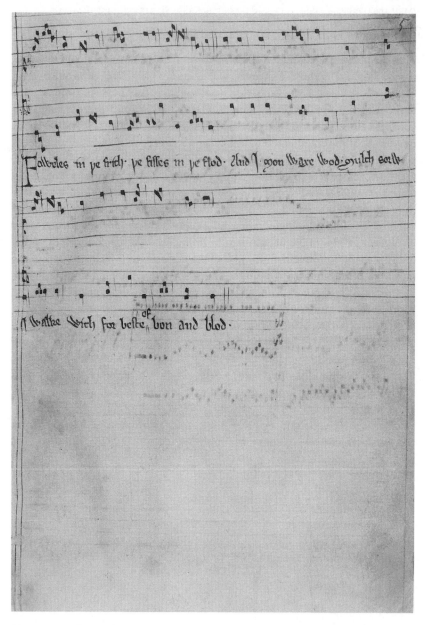

Figure 4   Bodleian Library MS Douce 139 (*SC* 21713), folio 5. This manuscript has been dated to about 1270, but the early and secular song it contains, "Foweles in the Frith" (no. 21), was no doubt composed 20 or more years earlier, possibly in East Anglia.

22

IMEV 1008. Bodleian Library, Oxford. MS Rawlinson D. 913 (*SC* 13679), fol. 1v (g). Davies no. 31. Duncan A no. 117. Robbins no. 15.

Another of the Rawlinson Lyrics, written as prose on the single strip of parchment about 1325, which, in its present form, may have been cut from a much larger, folio leaf (see figure 3, p. 75). It contains, *inter alia*, unique texts of "Maiden in the mor lay" (no. 20) and "Al night by the rose, Rose," (no. 38). The poem may be a kind of primitive (or perhaps simply an incomplete) carol, and seems more or less obviously suited to the dance. The first three lines are often read as a burden or refrain. The voice is that of a woman, possibly calling forth a man to come from a circle, or a press, and dance with her; it is not impossible that the author was a woman too. Yeats adapted the poem to a twentieth-century political context, setting what he took to be a call to idealism and engagement against modern man who prefers his comfort, and indeed there seems to be more to the poem than the lines declare, something which seems to call the auditor to a dance whose end is uncertain, whose purpose a mystery.

This poem, along with nos 20 and 38, are treated in Boklund-Lagopoulou, "*I have a yong suster*" (2002) and in J. A. Burrow, "Poems without Contexts: The Rawlinson Lyrics," cited under no. 20, above.

Ich am of Irlaunde,
Ant of the holy londe
Of Irlande.

Ich = I; of = from
Ant = and

Gode sire, preye Ich the,
For of saynte charite
Come ant daunce wyt me
In Irlaunde.

trans. = for (the sake) of holy charity

23

Supplement 1356.3. Bodleian Library, Oxford. MS Laud Misc. 210 (*SC* 1292), fol. 1v.

This lyric, one from a relatively small group of poems which deal with the religious life, is like certain lyrics concerned with Mary's virginity in that it turns upon a series of paradoxes which hide the poem's meaning until its significance is suddenly revealed in the last line. Employing identical rhyme to emphasize youth and life in the first two lines, the poem invokes the theme of the *homo viator*, in which humankind is, on this earth, on pilgrimage, but presents the end of that pilgrimage as a place where death, fear, poverty, and contention do not exist. It echoes numerous scriptural passages, many of which link faith and life together, including: "I am the resurrection and the life: he that believeth in me, although he be dead, shall live" (Jn. 11.25), "I am the way, and the truth and the life" (Jn. 14.6), and "For he is not the God of the dead, but of the living: for all live to him" (Lk. 20.38).

The poem has been inserted as prose on what is now the first free folio, which was formerly pasted onto the front board, of a manuscript of 187 folios which contains several Middle English prose works of spiritual guidance. The first two of these are attributed to the fourteenth-century English mystic, Richard Rolle (though only the first, *The Form of Living*, is actually his). Some of Rolle's lyrics are printed in Appendix B, below, and it is possible that whoever added this lyric into the Laud manuscript either wrote or inserted it as a commentary on his life. Believing that the final *-e* has been lost from its unstressed position, perhaps for metrical convenience, I have printed *lede* in the last line, a simple present verb ("thus I lead my life"), though the manuscript reading is *led*, a past tense, which is only possible if the narrator is intended suddenly to reveal that she or he is speaking from the grave, as is possible if the poem was intended to reflect, or pay tribute to, Richard Rolle. First printed by me in *English Language Notes* 17 (1980): 163–5.

I seche a youthe that eldyth noght,	*eldyth noght = does not grow old*
I seche a lyf that dyeth noght,	
I seche joye withowte drede,	
I seche richesse withowte nede,	*nede = need*
I seche ful blisse withowte strife,	
And therfore thus I lede my lyf.	*lede = lead (or led?)*

24

IMEV 1132. Balliol College, Oxford. MS 354, fol. 165v. Davies no. 164. Duncan B no. 79. Greene no. 322A.

This carol, written down early in the sixteenth century in a manuscript which also contains nos. 11 and 47, seems intended both to reveal and to obscure its meaning, and to do both more or less at the same time. While it is not difficult to assign "meanings" to several of its various elements, part of its intention seems finally *not* to reveal all of its significance, but to leave its central topic, the even greater mystery of the Eucharist, unresolved and so susceptible to a sense of wonder and the sacred which is imbedded in any spiritual quest, for the Holy Grail, for Christ himself. The feast of Corpus Christi, celebrating the institution of the sacrament of the Eucharist on Holy Thursday, was begun by Pope Urban IV in 1264, and was widely known and celebrated throughout late medieval England.

Thus whatever the meaning and effect of its symbolism, the poem is emphatically a Corpus Christi carol, in which the "hall" represents the Castle of the Grail, the knight the wounded keeper of the Grail, the "mayden," the Grail maiden, who laments Christ's death, and the falcon and the stone constituent parts of that sacred mystery. There has also been an attempt (to me unconvincing) by Richard L. Greene (*Medium Aevum*, 29 (1960): 10–21) to assign a political reading to the poem, with the falcon representing Anne Boleyn, King Henry VIII's wife, whose badge was a white falcon. The poem is also treated by Boklund-Lagopoulou, *"I have a yong suster"* (2002), and Oliver, *Poems Without Names* (1970).

Lully, lully, lully, lully,
The fawcon hath born my mak away.   *mak = mate, lover*

He bare hym vp, he bare hym down,
He bare hym into an orchard brown.

Lully, lully . . .

In that orchard ther was an hall,
That was hangid with purpill and pall.   *purpill and pall = heavy purple draperies*

Lully, lully . . .

And in that hall ther was a bed,
Hit was hangid with gold so rede.

Lully, lully . . .

And yn that bed ther lythe a knyght,   *lythe = lies*
His wowndes bledyng day and nyght.

Lully, lully . . .

By that bedes side ther kneleth a may,   *may = maiden*
And she wepeth both nyght and day.

Lully, lully . . .

And by that beddes side ther stondith a ston,
Corpus Christi wretyn theron.   trans. = The Body of Christ

Lully, lully . . .

This version of the poem just above (no. 24) circulated widely, and in the nineteenth century other, and no doubt later, versions were recorded by students of
folklore and folk music. It is difficult to know how far back these versions reach,
but taken together they seem to indicate that the derived versions of this carol
were usually identified with Christ's Nativity and/or Passion and with the
Eucharist, and not with any political theme connected to Henry VIII. But it is
also evident from these derived versions that the poem's meaning was understood to contain mystery and to evoke wonder – or at least incomprehension.
One of these nineteenth-century versions was recorded in Derbyshire; the third
stanza is cited from the fourth stanza of another version, Greene 322B, which
ignores the Eucharistic symbolism connoted in the image of blood, and includes
in its place a somewhat grotesque stanza in which the evident symbolic notation is abandoned in favor of what may simply have been an empirical obser-
vation: "At that bed's foot there lies a hound,/Which is licking the blood as it
daily runs down." These later versions indicate the modern course of many a
medieval song.

Nineteenth-century Derbyshire Version, Greene 322C
  Down in yon forest there stands a hall,
  The bells of Paradise, I heard them ring.
  It's covered all over with purple and pall,
  And I love my Lord Jesus above anything.

In that hall there stands a bed,
The bells, etc.
It's covered all over with scarlet and red,
And I love, etc.

[And in that bed there lies a knight,
Whose wounds do bleed by day and by night.]

At the bedside there lies a stone,
Which the sweet Virgin Mary knelt upon.

Under that bed there runs a flood,
The one half runs water, the other runs blood.

At the bed's foot there grows a thorn,
Which ever blows blossom since he was born.

Over that bed the moon shines bright,
Denoting our Savior was born this night.

VI

Poems about Christ's Life and Passion

The image of the human Christ which appears in medieval English lyrics can sometimes seem so apparently "modern" as to require little if any critical comment, but often too it encodes religious and even theological teachings which would have been understood by contemporaries, but are now largely unfamiliar. Nowhere is this more true than in the representation of his human and divine natures, certainly the most important medieval teaching concerning the way Christ was understood during this period, and a continuing and powerful theological attitude in perhaps the majority of lyrics associated with his death. Since the Council of Chalcedon in 451 AD, it was accepted as orthodox teaching of the medieval church, East and West alike, that Christ had two "natures," one human and one divine, and that they were joined together in hypostatic ("in substance") union. This meant that one nature neither became absorbed in, nor did it in any way take precedence over, the other, but together they were joined in one person, Jesus Christ. Difficulties arose with the translation of the Greek theological concept into Latin, in which one word, *substantia*, had to signify two different Greek concepts, that of a general and of a specific nature. Chalcedon sought to clarify these usages by identifying in Christ both a divine son and a real person, two natures, one human and one divine; and it refused to let the term "nature" apply to his divine nature alone. Christ's humanity was, in this teaching, as important as his divinity. In the following centuries the teaching informed the doctrine both of the Trinity and of the Incarnation, and in the late medieval period it was examined and commented upon by theologians as different as Thomas Aquinas (c.1225–74) and Duns Scotus (c.1265–1308), even while the traditional formulation persisted.

This doctrine had particular importance for poets, even though few developed it expressly in their work, because it taught that Christ was both truly human, and could thus in his life both love and suffer pain (he was not, in his human nature, "impassible," unable to feel either pleasure or pain, as Greek thought had taught of God), but at the same time he was truly God, perfect, immutable, and all-sufficient. In many poems and in other texts too it is the human nature of Christ which appears most vividly, and some contain non-doctrinal folk beliefs, such as the one which held that, because Christ had no human father, his suffering during the Passion was greater than anyone had ever endured. These texts focused on Christ's human nature, but, notwithstanding Church teaching, saw it as being in some way informed by his divine, so that the most extra-ordinary attributes could be attached to him without contradiction. But other texts held firmly to the doctrine that Christ was God in the complex way I have described, and these in particular could realize, sometimes powerfully, a representation of Christ which depended on an understanding of his two natures. The importance of this doctrine was understood from earliest times (in part because of the heresy of Nestorius, bishop of Constantinople, 428–31 (d. c.451), who was thought to have taught that there were two separate persons, not two natures, in Christ) and an early work by Cyril of Alexandria (d. 444), *On the Unity of Christ*, made the teaching relatively well known. In late medieval England, it was usually assumed, at least where it was understood.

I have tried in this part to indicate, through the lyrics, some aspects of late medieval religiousness and spirituality – the Christian's engagement with an image of God which is both joyful and finally stabilizing but often demand-ing and sometimes unyielding, a tortured and human-like divinity, but one which does not cease to be unknowable and absolute. The secondary literature on so broad a topic is enormous, but there is a good overview of the visual evidence in Gertrud Schiller's *Iconography of Christian Art*, 2 volumes, trans. Janet Seligman (Greenwich, Conn.: New York Graphic Society, Ltd, 1972); volume 2 concerns only the Passion, volume 1 everything that took place in Christ's life before. Perhaps the single greatest religious topic in the late medieval period was Christ's Passion, and there is an instructive treatment based on evidence from the Low Countries (which informed English texts) in James H. Marrow, *Passion Iconography in Northern European Art of the Late Middle Ages and Renaissance: A Study of the Transformation of Sacred Metaphor into Descriptive Narrative*, Ars Neerlandica volume 1 (Kortrijh, Belgium: Van Ghemmert Publishing Co., 1979), useful in particular for its study of "The Secret Passion," pp. 95–170, non-gospel narra-tives which became attached to the story of Christ's Passion, often based upon scriptural passages not associated with it directly. There is a good collection of essays on the subject of Christ's Passion edited by A. A. MacDonald, et al., *The Broken Body: Passion Devotion in Late-Medieval Culture*, Mediaevalia Groningana vol. XXI (Groningen: Egbert Forsten, 1998). Christ's body and the human body generally are now much treated in studies of medieval culture, see in particu-lar, Sarah Beckwith, *Christ's Body: Identity, Culture and Society in Late Medieval Writings* (London and New York: Routledge, 1993), and Sarah Kay and Miri Rubin, eds.,

Framing Medieval Bodies (Manchester: University of Manchester Press, and New York: St Martin's Press, 1996).

More specifically, there is an account of the kinds of religiousness found in Middle English lyrics in David L. Jeffrey, "Forms of Spirituality in the Middle English Lyric," in *Imagination and the Spirit: Essays in Literature and the Christian Faith Presented to Clyde S. Kilby* (Grand Rapids, Mich.: William B. Eerdmans Publishing Company, 1971), pp. 55–85, and especially in Douglas Gray, "Popular Religion and Late Medieval Literature," in Piero Boitani and Anna Torti, eds., *Religion in the Poetry and Drama of the Late Middle Ages in England*, The J. A. W. Bennett Memorial Lectures (Cambridge: D. S. Brewer, 1990), pp. 1–28, and for an account as to how such poems were often read by the Christian in prayer, see my "Prayer and Meditation in Late Medieval England: MS Bodley 789," *Medium Aevum* 48 (1979): 55–66. For a study of the implications of Mary's role in lyrics on the Passion see Sarah Stanbury, "The Virgin's Gaze: Spectacle and Transgression in Middle English Lyrics of the Passion," *PMLA* 106 (1991): 1083–93.

There is an English translation of *On the Unity of Christ* by John Anthony McGuckin (Crestwood, N.Y.: St Vladimir's Seminary, 1995), and an admirable account of the dogmas and teachings concerning Christ's human nature in the late medieval period by Richard Cross, *The Metaphysics of the Incarnation: Thomas Aquinas to Duns Scotus* (Oxford and New York: Oxford University Press, 2002).

25

IMEV 29. Bodleian Library, Oxford. MS Bodley 26 (*SC* 1871), fol. 202v.
Greene no. 12.

Appropriately embedded in a stout parchment codex written about 1350 which contains a collection of early fourteenth-century sermons, this carol complexly reads the Passion into the Nativity, part of the powerful medieval Christian dynamic which saw both joy and pain together as an integral part of human life, whether on a sacred or a secular level. The ways in which Christ was understood and realized had great variety, though they all rested on the teaching (discussed above) that he was God, but God become man. The Nativity was important precisely because it marked the point at which the promise of the Annunciation was fulfilled, but it pointed as well toward Christ's suffering, death, and (though this was not always emphasized or even realized in the lyrics) resurrection. It sometimes seems as though, to the persona of this poem, joy without suffering is somehow incomplete, or perhaps that suffering is waiting, at least on this earth, just on the other side of joy.

Honnd by honnd we schulle ous take,
And ioye and blisse schulle we make,
For the deuel of ele man haght forsake   ele = hell; haght forsake = hath forsaken
And Godes Son ys maked oure make.   make = companion, lover

A child is boren amonges man,
And in that child was no wam.   wam = blemish
That child ys God, that child is man,
And in that child oure lif bygan.

Honnd by honnd . . .

Senful man, be blithe and glad,   Senful = sinful; blithe = happy
For your mariage thy peys ys grad,   peys ys grad = peace is announced
Wan Crist was boren.
Com to Crist, thy peis ys grad,
For the was hys blod yshed
That were forloren.

Honnd by honnd . . .

Senful man, be blithe and bold,
For heuene is bothe boght and sold,

Euereche fote.   trans. = *every foot*
Com to Crist, thy peys is told,
For the he gahf a hondrefold   *gahf = gave*
Hys lif to bot.   *to bot = as salvation*

26

IMEV 196. Windsor, Eton College. MS 36, fol. 238. Brown B no. 49.

This fine if complex fourteenth-century poem moves in quite another direction than the last one. It initially sounds the theme of changeless divine love which is found in Mary, provocatively adding, "but more" in Christ, as it reminds its reader that Christ's grace springs from and works through his love for humankind, while at the same time responding to the implied question as to where true and unvarying love may be found. The poem brilliantly and unusually represents human failure in turning away from Christ, which it equates not only with sin but also with human imperfection, an imperfection, however, which the Christian can amend by responding to the prompting of divine grace. It further implies that doubt and uncertainty are, or can be, a part of the Christian life, and ambiguously contrasts the free acceptance of divine love itself with what the Christian has come to expect from Rome, and so from the institutional church, which it clearly implies is not as powerful or as important as what Christ's own love and freely given grace ("Crist me founde") will surely bring. This last detail, important though it is, is touched upon gracefully, almost in passing, and does not seem to have been *per se* the "point" of the lyric.

The reference to Rome is made all the more piquant by the fact that the poem is uniquely preserved as a late and informal addition to a large fourteenth-century composite manuscript, Eton College MS 36, which contains, in the section which preserves the lyric, certain of the writings not only of Vegetius (as Brown noted), but also of St. Thomas Aquinas (1225–74). In its allusion to Rome, however, and perhaps in that to Christ's primacy over Mary, the lyric seems very possibly to echo, but not finally to endorse, certain aspects of Lollard teaching, though it seems to have been inscribed before such teachings were universally regarded as heretical, at a time when some form of accommodation could still have been envisioned with the institutional church. In this context, the allusion to Rome appears to record the importance of the way in which the Christian, responding to divine grace, can rise to a new and direct understanding of the love between God and humankind. But it is also difficult to escape the impression that the poem was inserted into the manuscript as a gentle correction to the teaching of St. Thomas, even though the saint was not yet as identified with orthodoxy as he later became. Or perhaps the poem stands counterpoint to the practice of scholastic philosophy generally, and seeks to remind its learned reader, whom the scribe would surely have expected to be his first (and perhaps only) audience, of the primacy of divine love.

The text as we have it requires three emendations, the first and third (lines 8 and 24) emended by Brown and more or less obvious, the second (line 9) entirely conjectural. Can you suggest an alternative to any or all of them?

Al other loue is lych the mone,   *lych = like; mone = moon*
That wext and wanet as flour   *wext and wanet = grows and decreases;*
 in plein,   *plein = plain*
As flour that fayret and fawyt sone,   *fayret and fawyt = flowers and fades*
As day that scwret and endt in rein.   *scwret = passes rapidly*

Al other love bigint bi blisse,
In wep and wo mak is hending,   *hending = ending*
No loue ther nis that over halle lysse,   *halle = all; lysse = solaces*
Bot wat areste in hevene kyng.   *Bot = MS omission; wat = what;*
    areste = rests

Wos love ys sure and eure grene,   *sure = MS omission; eure = ever*
And eure ful wythoute wayyng,   *wayyng = waining*
Is love suetyth wythoute tene,   *suetyth = sweetens; tene = suffering*
Is love is hendles and aring.   *hendles = endless; aring = unfailing*

Al other love Y flo for the,   *flo = forsake, flee*
Tel me, tel me, wer thou lyst.   *wer thou lyst = where you may be found*
"In Marie mylde an fre   *fre = gracious*
I schal be fonde, ak mor in Crist."   *ak mor = but more*

Crist me founde, noght Y the, hast,
Hald me to the wiht al thi meyn,   *wiht = with; meyn = force, power*
Help, geld that mi love be stedfast,   *geld = grant, requite*
Lest thus sone it turne ageyn.

Wan nou yet myn hert is sore,   *yet = MS hyt; trans. = when my heart is yet sore*
Ywys hie spilt myn herte blod,   *Ywys = indeed, certainly*
God canne mi lef, Y care na mor,   *canne = knows; lef = love; na mor = no more*
Yet Y hope his wil be good.   *Yet = MS hyt*

Alas, what wole Y a Rome?
Seye Y may in lore of loue,   *Seye = speak; lore = teaching*
"Vndo Y am by manne dome,   *manne dome = human fate*
Bot he me help that syt aboue."   *Bot = unless*

27

IMEV 4141. Trinity College Cambridge. MS 323 (B.14.39/40), fol. 83v. Brown A no. 34.

This powerful thirteenth-century poem moves from the intellectual apprehension of Christ as God of the previous poems to an affective realization of Christ's Passion which centers upon an imagined and detailed image of Christ, his side opened, his back beaten raw, and his head crowned with thorns, standing between Mary and John. This is quite an early representation for such a graphic image (which would become common a century later), and even now, to any who read it meditatively, it is not without a certain devotional and psychological power. There were shorter poems as well, such as no. 28, below, which assumed rather than developed the kind of meditative introspection indicated here, and sought to construct a devotional aesthetic rooted in a felt remembrance of Christ's Passion. Such powerful and devout poems were widely known and deeply rooted, and, changes both theological and literary having been made, flowered in the seventeenth century in the hands of such very different masters as George Herbert (1593–1633) and Richard Crashaw (1613–49).

Wose seye on rode,	*Wose seye = whoever saw; rode = cross*
Ihesus is lefman,	*is = his; lefman = lover*
Sory stod him bi wepinde	*wepinde = weeping*
Sent Marie and Sent Jon,	
His hewid him al abutun	*hewid = head; al abutun = all about*
Wid thornis i-prikit,	*Wid = with; i-prikit = pricked*
Is faire hondin and is waire wed	*waire wed = fair feet*
Wid naylis y-stickit,	*y-stickit = pierced, stuck*
Is rug wid yerdis suonken	*rug = back; yerdis = rods*
Is syde wid sper y-vundit,	*y-vundit = wounded*
Al for sunne of mon,	*sunne = sin*
Sore he may wepin,	*wepin = weep*
And bittre teris letin,	*letin = let fall*
Mon thad of luue con.	*thad = that; luue = love; con = knows, can*

28

IMEV 2507. Trinity College, Cambridge. MS 1157 (O.2.53), fol. 69.
Davies no. 79. Duncan B no. 69. Gray no. 26(b).

This short, hard, popular poem echoes the meditative and devotional voice of
the last one, but depends almost entirely on its reader's intellectual predisposi-
tion and prepared habits of mind in order to realize its finally contextual power.
It appears in three manuscripts beside an illustration of Christ as the suffering
"Man of Sorrows," the *imago pietatis*, with five (or many) wounds, with much
blood clearly visible – as an example of this practice, see figure 5, p. 95. Post-
Reformation art would come to limit the amount of blood associated with Christ's
Passion, but medieval art did not, and representations of Christ suffering were
often accompanied by a crown of thorns, a sepulcher, three nails, and a cross.
Such treatments often proceed without recourse to any but the most basic scriptural reference, and seem deliberately to avoid natural, literary, or liturgical
allusion in a quick movement to engage the reader's affections. The final line
of this poem represents Christ as literally holding out his heart to the reader in
meditation, an image present in Additional MS 37049 and in numerous other
manuscript illustrations. Another more widely known poem, *IMEV* 1703, exists
in 18 versions, and, with its clanging rhyme and simple theology, lent itself to
memorization. Its first four lines were often incorporated into other devotional
poems, and Bodleian Library, Oxford MS Rawlinson Liturg. f. 36, an elegant
little manuscript formerly belonging to the Talbot family, announces the poem,
in red, as "A deuote prayer," and presents its short text thus on folio 63v:

> Ihesu, for thy holy name,
> And for they bitter passion,
> Saue vs fro synne and shame,
> And endless dampnacion.
> And bryng vs to that blysse,
> That never shall haue end.
> Swete Ihesu, Amen.

For many, simple, short prayer-poems like this one summarized an important
aspect of their interior spirituality, and seem to have informed their understanding
of their faith. More complex lyrics, however, presented a finally more complicated development of that belief, even while remaining attached theologically
to these less sophisticated formulations.

On the lyric which follows below, see Thomas W. Ross, "Five Fifteenth-Century
'Emblem' Verses from Brit. Mus. Addit. MS 37049," *Speculum* 32 (1957): 274–82,
for a compelling description of one such illustrated Carthusian manuscript in which
the poem appears, and see also the two articles by Rossell Hope Robbins cited

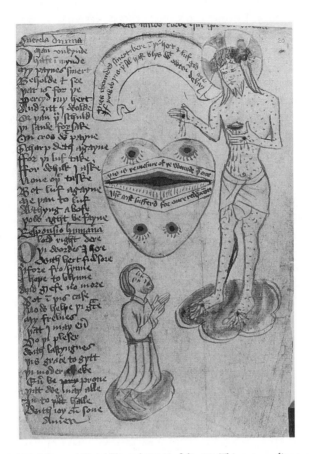

Figure 5   British Library MS Additional 37049, folio 20. This extraordinary manuscript was produced at an unidentified Carthusian charterhouse in northern England, probably between 1460 and 1470. It contains a wide variety of extracts from the religious, devotional, and moral literature of late medieval England, and is illustrated with 145 brightly colored, effective, but crude drawings. Here it shows Christ, spotted with drops of his own blood (the number of these, divinely revealed, was traditionally held to be 28,430, or according to a later version, 547,500); they fell from the many wounds Christ received in his Passion (conventionally, around about 5,475 separate wounds; there were medieval devotions which involved invoking each of them). Christ is shown standing before a kneeling penitent whom he enjoins: "Thies woundes smert [painful] bere in thi hert and luf God aye [ever]. Yf thou do this thou sul haf [shall have] blys withowten delay" (*Supplement* 3560.5). He faces a Middle English prayer-poem (*IMEV* 2504; Brown C no. 108). Between them is a drawing of Christ's "Five Wounds," another familiar medieval devotion, here represented by a conventional drawing of his heart, pierced by Longinus' spear, and containing representations of the holes made in his hands and feet by the four nails which held him to the cross. The inscription reads: "This is the mesure [size] of the wounde that our [Lord: *omitted*] Ihu Crist sufferd for oure redempcion." The spirituality both represented and encoded in these illustrations informed, often indirectly, many late medieval English lyrics, including several published here, but see in particular no. 28.

under no. 4, above. Devotion to Christ's blood was embedded in the English Passion lyric, and may have been informed by the 1247 gift of a relic of Christ's blood to Westminster Abbey by King Henry III (1207–72, reigned 1216–72); on that donation see Nicholas Vincent, *The Holy Blood: King Henry III and the Westminister Blood Relic* (Cambridge: Cambridge University Press, 2001). Woolf points out (p. 186) that the poem could have had a secular connotation to complement its evident religious significance, and reflect the "exchange of hearts" which takes place between lovers, and so appears in countless secular texts, then as now. See Woolf, *The English Religious Lyric in the Middle Ages* (1968).

O man vnkynde
Have thow yn mynde   *yn mynde = in meditation*
My passyon smert.   *smert = sharp*

Thow shalst me fynde
To thee full kynde:
Lo, here my hert!   *here = here [is]* (with a pun on hear?)

29

London. MS Lambeth Palace 78, fol. 223v, column 2.

It is probably only by reading the last two poems (or texts like them) that the reader can understand the five simple yet felt couplets which, in a kind of dramatic dialogue, make up this lyric. Lyrics can sometimes be found embedded in Middle English dramas, but, unusually, this poem seems to have been conceived of as a kind of dramatic exchange, one now overheard by the reader. It opens with a prayer of a virgin to Christ (6 lines), which is followed by a lament of the devil (4 lines), which makes clear that the virgin's prayer has been answered. Drops of blood function here, as elsewhere in the canon, as tokens of Christ's love.

The poem was first published by Siegfried Wenzel, in "Unrecorded Middle English Verses," *Anglia* 92 (1974): 55–78, this poem appeared on page 65.

[A maiden speaks, perhaps on the verge of entering a religious order:]
Ihesu, my spowse good and trewe,
Ne take me to noon other newe,   *noon other newe = no other new thing*
In thy kepyng I me betake,
And the I haue chose to my make.   *make = companion, lover*
Som tokyn of loue thow send me blyue,   *blyue = quickly*
That I the fend away may dryue.   *fend = fiend, devil*

[The devil speaks:]
Alas, alas, I am ynome,   *ynome = taken, beaten*
A woman me hath ouyrcome.
Sethe I on here se Crystys blod,   *Sethe = since*
For fere I fle and wax wood.   *fere = fear; wax wood = go mad*

30

This poem gives further evidence that the poets who inscribed these lyrics included in their number agile and witty clerks, sometimes still at university, who were engaged, *inter alia*, in the study of philosophy. This lyric begins each stanza with a Latin tag reminiscent of the introduction to a definition present in a medieval philosophy textbook, but then adds a sharp and fresh definition of the cause, associated here (not in the textbooks!) with Christ's Passion. In scholastic philosophy, the Four Causes are usually distinguished thus: the Material Cause is that from which something is produced; the Efficient Cause is the agent which causes the change; the Formal Cause is the specific element in a being which communicates itself to a less determinate being and so gives it form; and the Final Cause is the final end or purpose toward which change is directed. But the topic here is Christ's Passion, and the definitions associated with its causes are brilliantly fresh and original. Balance and opposition figure prominently in even the least polished of lyrics, like these lines preserved in the same manuscript, folio 121 verso, in which Christ's Passion is presented as the remedy both for our sin, and for our (spiritual) illness: "Crist ys wounded for oure wikkednesse, / And we buth ful heled of oure sikness." But the poem which follows is even more playfully sophisticated.

First published by Theo Stemmler, "More English Texts from MS Cambridge University Library Ii.III.8," *Anglia* 93 (1975): 1–16, poem on p. 11. For extended scholastic definitions see Bernard Wuellner, SJ, *Dictionary of Scholastic Philosophy* (Milwaukee: Bruce Publishing Co., 1956).

Causa materialis huius rubricacionis est:
A body tender of complexion
And nobelyst in kynde.

trans. = the material cause of this rubrication is
complexion = *constitution*
kynde = *nature*

Causa efficiens est:
A pepulle wyckyd of condicioun,
And of alle men most vnkynde.

trans. = the efficient cause is
pepulle = *people*

Causa formalis est:
Scharpe and schamefull.

trans. = the formal cause is

Causa finalis:
Best and blisfull.

trans. = the final cause

VII

Poems Inviting or Disparaging Love

As the secular lyric developed, the poet's imaginative engagement not only with his or her beloved, but also with an event or a series of events which may or may not have taken place, became central to the English love lyric. On the continent there were two powerful poetic genres, the *aubade* and the pastoral, which concerned themselves with, and so represented, the trials of two usually young lovers. In the *aubade* both the meeting and the parting of the lovers were prearranged, and so are expected by participants and audience alike; not so, as Dronke points out, in the pastoral, where chance and sheer coincidence can play a role, and where the meeting takes place in the open. In the *aubade* the lovers are already one, often physically. The pastoral is more likely to represent a struggle or a seduction, with the man often represented as coming from a higher social class than the young woman whom he addresses.

These conventions were well established on the continent, and specifically informed the English love lyric, which, however, since it often both originated in and was preserved by noble or courtly audiences (and manuscripts), usually avoided close adherence to the details of those traditional conventions. Still, when reading or listening to the following poems, it is probably a good idea to notice not only the attitudes but also the circumstances within which the exchange between the lovers is taking place. There was in English lyrics (as in other literary arts) a tendency to treat empirically situations, attitudes, and even ideas which in Europe would have been understood to have been conventional. But in Middle English lyrics this is not necessarily the case, and English poetic practices can lend an air of freshness and (when required) grace to otherwise conventional literary and lyrical attitudes.

Thus, when reading love lyrics, whether secular or sacred, it is good to ask where the poem seems to be taking place, and whether any putative "depth of feeling" which may be involved seems to you purely conventional or otherwise constrained by social or poetic tradition. The presence of a conventional utterance will not of course invalidate or render "insincere" any sentiment, since such language was one of a number of poetic practices available to the poet, but it may complicate your understanding of it. Has a "past history" been stated or implied in the lyric? What are the intentions of either party, and in what ways – by voice or tone, for example – are they communicated to the reader? Are any artifacts alluded to? What values may be expressed or implied?

General studies of the medieval lyric in England and on the continent are relatively rare, but even after 25 years Peter Dronke's excellent book *The Medieval Lyric*, third edition (1996) repays rereading; in the context of this discussion, see especially "The Alba," chapter 5, pp. 167–85. See too T. J. B. Spencer's study of the English *aubade* in his contribution to Arthur T. Hatto, ed., *Eos: An Enquiry into the Theme of Lovers' Meetings and Partings at Dawn in Poetry* (London, The Hague, Paris: Mouton, 1965), pp. 505–53. Rossell Hope Robbins has written about the courtly and noble associations and manuscripts of the lyrics in "The Middle English Court Love Lyric," in W. T. H. Jackson, ed., *The Interpretation of Medieval Lyric Poetry* (New York: Columbia University Press, 1980), pp. 205–32, and Richard Firth Green has detailed the literary associations of the English court in *Poets and Princepleasers: Literature and the English Court in the Late Middle Ages* (Toronto, Buffalo, and London: University of Toronto Press, 1980). Exceptionally, the manuscripts of English court lyrics have been examined in a perceptive study by Julia Boffey, *Manuscripts of English Courtly Love Lyrics in the Later Middle Ages*, Manuscript Studies 1 (Cambridge: D. S. Brewer, 1985).

31

IMEV 515. British Library, London. Harley MS 2253, fol. 63v. Brown A no. 77. Davies no. 13. Duncan A no. 18.

Although in some respects already conventional, the description of setting and woman in this thirteenth-century poem already records many of the love-lyric conventions familiar in later centuries, but it does so with a freshness and a verve not always present in the later poems. It also seems charged with a degree of sexual energy which runs throughout, concluding with the almost modern sentiment that it is better to have loved and lost than never to have loved at all – besides, one's luck might always change. There is a useful study of this lyric among others in John F. Plummer, III, "The Poetic Function of Conventional Language in the Middle English Lyric," *Studies in Philology* 72 (1975): 367–85.

Bytuene Mersh ant Aueril,   *trans.* = *between March and April*
When spray biginneth to springe,   *spray* = *branch*
The lutel foul hath hire wyl   *lutel foul* = *little fowl*
On hyre lud to synge.   *On hyre lud* = *in her voice*
Ich libbe in loue-longinge   *Ich libbe* = *I live*
For semlokest of alle thynge.   *semlokest . . . thynge* = *fairest thing there is*
He may me blisse bringe,   *He* = *she*
Ich am in hire baundoun.   *in hire baundoun* = *under her power*

An hendy hap i-chabbe y-hent,   *trans.* = *a lucky chance I have got*
Ich ot from hevene it is me sent,   *ot* = *wot, know*
From alle wymmen my love is lent,   *lent* = *gone*
And lyht on Alysoun.

On heu hire her is fayr ynoh,   *trans.* = *of hue her hair is fair enough*
Hir browe broune, hire eyen blake,   *eyen* = *eyes;* MS *eye*
With lossum chere he on me loh,   *lossom chere* = *lovely face; he* = *she; loh* = *smiled*
With middel smal and wel ymake.
Bote he me wolle to hire take   *Bote* = *unless; he* = *she*
For te ben hire owen make,   *te* = *to; make* = *lover*
Longe to lyuen I shulle forsake,
And feye fallen adoun.   *feye* = *doomed*

An hendy hap . . .

Nihtes when I wende and wake,   *wende = toss*
For to myn wonges waxeth   *wonges = cheeks; waxeth = grow;*
   won,   *won = wan, pale*
Leuedi, al for thine sake,
Longinge is ylent me on.   *ylent me on = come upon me*
In world nis non so wyter mon   *wyter mon = wise a man*
That al hire bounte telle con.   *telle con = can tell*
Hire swyre is whittore then the swon,   *swyre = neck; swon = swan*
And feyrest may in toune.   *may = maiden*

An hendy hap . . .

Ich am for wowyng al forwake,   *wowing = making love; forwake = exhausted*
Wery so water in wore.   *so = as; wore = pool*
Lest eny reue me my make   *reue = take from; make = love*
Ich abbe y-yerned yore.   *abbe = have; yore = so long*
Betere is tholien whyle sore   *tholien = to suffer; sore = in pain*
Then mournen euermore.
Geynest vnder gore,   *trans. = kindest in gown*
Herkne to my roun.   *roun = speech, poem*

An hendy hap . . .

32

IMEV 927. Bodleian Library, Oxford. MS Douce 326 (*SC* 21900), fol. 14–14v. Brown C no. 46. Davies no. 105. Duncan B no. 51.

At first reading this poem seems unexceptional, but its apparently conventional language and imagery carry with it a degree of conviction which are at once literary and emotional, and which lend energy and even meaning to a lyric which, in one reading at least, begins as one kind of poem, but ends as another. The language at the end seems not to be in conflict with the implied eroticism of the early verses, so that it is possible to read the poem either as a religious lyric in praise of the Blessed Virgin, or as a secular love lyric in praise of the poet's beloved. Is the inexpressibility *topos* present because of the beloved's beauty, or because she is, quite literally, a sainted and so a divine person? In either case, love between human beings is here represented, in a decidedly medieval way, as a reflection of the love which exists between God and humankind. Still, the poem itself must be either sacred or secular; it cannot be both. But which is it? Why?

At line 30 the manuscript reads "she" when "he" might be expected. I have preserved that reading, which comes at the point when the religious nature of the poem becomes clear, and so may possibly indicate the poet adding to the surprise of the moment by revealing her own gender. I owe the emendation in line 23 ("Wy" for MS "Wyll") to Brown.

Goe, lytyll byll, and doe me recommende	*byll = letter*
Vnto my lady, with godely countynaunce,	
For, trusty messanger, I the sende.	
Pray her that she make puruyaunce	*puruyaunce = provision*
For my loue, thurgh here sufferaunce,	*here sufferaunce = her permision*
In her bosome desyreth to reste,	
Syth off all women, I loue here beste.	*Syth = since*
She ys lylly off redolence,	*redolence = fragrance*
Wych only may doe me plesure.	
She is the rose off conffydence,	
Most conffortyng to my nature.	
Vnto that lady I me assure.	*me assure = commit myself*
I wyll hur loue and neuer mo:	*neuer mo = no other*
Goe, lytyll byll, and sey hur so.	
She resteth in my remembraunce	*resteth = MS restyd*
Day other nyght, wherso I be.	*other = and*

It ys my specyall dalyaunce   *dalyaunce = delight*
For to remembyr hur bewte.
She is enprentyd in ych degre   *ych = each*
With yftes of nature inexplycable,
And eke of grace incomparable.   *eke = also*

The cause therfor, yf she wyll wytt,   *wytt = know*
Wy I presume on sych a flower,   *Wy = why; MS Wyll*
Say off hyr, for yt ys iwrytt,   *iwrytt = written (here)*
She is the feyrest paramour,   *paramour = lover*
And to man in ych langour   *ych langour = every illness*
Most souerayne medyatryce.   *medyatryce = mediator*
Therffor I loue that flowre of pryce.

Her bewte holy to dyscryve   *holy = wholly*
Who is she that may ssuffyce?   *she = thus MS; some read he*
For soth, no clerk that is on lyve,
Syth she is only withowtyn vyce.
Her flauour excedith the Flowr-de-lyce,   *Flowr-de-lyce = fleur-de-lys*
Afore all flowres I haue hur chose
Enterely in myn herte to close.

Hyr I beseche, seth I not feyne   *feyne = pretend*
Butt only putt me in hur grace,
That off me she not dysdeyne,
Takinge regarde at old trespace.
Seth myn entent in euery place
Shal be to doe hur obeysaunce,
And hur to loue saunce varyaunce.   *saunce = sans, without*

33

IMEV 1303. British Library, London. MS Sloane 2593, fol. 11–11v. Davies no. 75. Duncan A no. 124. Robbins no. 45.

See figure 2, p. 39. Sometimes associated with riddling poems or with rhymes for children, this poem in fact transcends the conventions of both genres, which helps to account for its extraordinarily wide distribution – as many as three related songs have been recorded in the United States. Although the correspondent is identified as a "sister," the word could have many meanings, and a tone of barely submerged separation and longing runs throughout. The poem draws the reader on with the quick engagement of music, posing questions soon to be answered, and anticipating a final answer which both surprises and responds to them all. The poem is discussed in Boklund-Lagopoulou, *"I have a yong suster"* (2002), Arthur K. Moore, *The Secular Lyric in Middle English* (1951), and Oliver, *Poems Without Names* (1970), and is rooted in a playful and lyrical impulse, which both charms and surprises.

I haue a yong suster,   *suster = sister, etc.*
Fer beyondyn the se,
Many be the drowryis   *drowryis = love tokens*
That che sente me.   *che = she*

Che sente me the cherye,
Withoutyn ony ston,
And so che ded the dowe, *the = MS omission; dowe = dove*
Withoutyn ony bon.   *bon = bone*

Sche sente me the brer *Sche = she; brer = briar, wild rose*
Withoutyn ony rynde,   *rynde = (thorny) bark*
Sche bad me loue my lemman,
Withoute longgyng.

How shuld ony cherye
Ben withoute ston?
And how shuld ony dowe
Ben withoute bon?

How shuld ony brer
Ben withoute rynde?
How shuld Y loue myn lemman
Without longyng?

Quan the cherye was a flour,   *Quan = when*
Than hadde it non ston.
Quan the dowe was an ey,   *ey = egg*
Than hadde it non bon.

Quan the brere was on-bred,   *on-bred = unborn, still a seed*
Than hadde it non rynd,
Quan the maydyn haght that she louit,   *haght that = has what*
Che is without longing.

34

IMEV 932. British Library, London. Royal MS 17 D vi, fol. 3. Robbins no. 95.

Decidedly erotic, but not only that, in its language, symbolism, and sentiment, this elegant and engaging little lyric exploits its conventional language in order to reveal a strength of sentiment within a conventional but bold setting. It was scribbled carefully but hastily on the end papers of the manuscript which preserves it in a late fifteenth-century hand. A modern note in the manuscript records that it contains the coat of arms of Joan, daughter of Richard Neville, Earl of Salisbury, after her marriage to William Fitz-Allen, eleventh Earl of Arundel (1438–87). This identification does not fix the author of the poem or the circumstances of its composition, but it does tie it, really quite firmly, to a noble audience.

Goo, lytell ryng, to that ylke suehte,	*suehte* = *sweet one*
That hath my herte in hyr demaeyne,	*demaeyne* = *possession*
And loke thou knell doune at hyr ffete	
Beschyng hyr she wold not dysdayene	
On hur smalle fyngerys the to streyne.	*streyne* = pun: *clasp, slip*
Than I wyll you sey boldly:	
"My master wold that he wer I."	

35

IMEV 3832. Bodleian Library, Oxford. MS Rawlinson poet. 36 (*SC* 14530), fol. 3v–4. Davies no. 140. Robbins no. 208.

Written by a woman? There are far more poems in Middle English attacking women than attacking men, but we have learned by now not to assume male authorship just because the text which concerns us is anonymous, and this one does its best to even the score. Indeed, its tone, diction, and voice seem to be of the sort which appear in modern "poetry slams." Note the play on the conventional description of beauty, here however applied to a man. First described by Rossell Hope Robbins, "Two Middle English Satiric Love Epistles," *Modern Language Review* 37 (1942): 415–21, this and the next poem have more recently been placed in an even larger context by Jan Ziolkowski, "Avatars of Ugliness in Medieval Literature," *Modern Language Review* 79 (1984): 1–20. But for a good study of the use of invective in this period, see Douglas Gray, "Rough Music: Some Early Invectives and Flytings," *Yearbook of English Studies* 14 (1984): 21–43.

To my trew loue and able,
(As the wedyr cok, he is stable)   *wedyr cok* = *weather vane in the figure of a cock*
Thys letter to hym be deliueryd:

Vnto you, most froward, this lettre I write,
Whych hath causyd me so longe in dyspayre.
The goodlynesse of your person is esye to   *endyte* = *pun: describe/indite*
 endyte,
For he leuyth nat that can youre persone appayre,   *appayre* = *deride*
So comly best shapyn, of feture most fayre,
Most fresch of contenaunce, euyn as an oule   *oule* = *owl*
Ys best and most fauoryd of ony odyr foule.   *ony odyr* = *any other*

Youre manly visage, shortly to declare,   *shortly to declare* = *put simply*
Youre forehed, mouth, and nose so flatte,
In short conclusyon, best lykened to an hare   *hare* = *hare, rabbit*
Of alle lyvyng thynges, saue only a catte.   *saue* = *except*
More wold I sey yf I wyst what,   *wyst* = *knew*
That swete vysage ful ofte is beshrewyd   *beshrewyd* = *cursed*
Whan I remembre of som baud so lewd.

The proporcion of your body comende wele me aught,
Fro the shulder down, behynde and beforn.
Yf alle the peyntours in a land togedyr were soght,   *peyntours* = *painters*

A worse coude they not portrey thogh alle they had it sworn –
Kepe wele your pacience thogh I sende you a skorne!
Your garmentes vpon you ful gayly they hynge,   *garmentes = clothes*
As it were an olde gose had a broke wynge.   *gose = goose*

Your thyghes mysgrowen, youre shankys mych worse,   *thyghes = thighs*
Whoso beholde your knees so crokyd,
As ych of hem bad odyr Crystes curse. *As = as if; ych = each; odyr = the other*
So go they outward, youre hammys ben hokyd,
Such a peyre chaumbrys I neuer on lokyd!   *chaumbrys = legs*
So vngoodly youre helys ye lyfte,   *helys = heels; lyfte = lift*
And youre feet ben crokyd, with euyl thryfte.   *thryfte = advantage, success*

Who myght haue the loue of so swete a wyght,   *wyght = creature*
She myght be ryght glad that euer was she born,
She that onys wold in a dark nyght
Renne for your loue tyl she had caught a thorn,
I wolde hyr no more harme but hangyd on the morn,
That hath ij good eyen and I chese here suche a make, *ij = two; eyen = eyes*
Or onys wold lyft vp here hole for youre sake!

Youre swete loue, wyth blody naylys: *blody = bloody*
Whych fedyth mo lyce than quaylys.   *mo = more; lyce = lice*

36

IMEV 2437. Bodleian Library, Oxford. MS Rawlinson poet. 36 (*SC* 14530), fol. 4–5. Robbins no. 209.

A reply to the previous poem, which hardly seems anachronistic to call sexist. Notice both the voice and the method of attack, first of all from authorities (Chaucer and Cicero), then from the conventions of physical descriptions, then from brute insult. The circumstances under which these poems were written is unknown – they would probably be fascinating, if discovered.

To you, dere herte, variant and mutable,
Lyke to Carybdis whych is vnstable:

Carybdis = *the whirlpool in Chaucer's*
Troilus and Criseyde (V, 644) of that name

O fresch floure, most plesant of pryse,
Fragrant as fedyrfoy to mannys inspeccion,
Me semyth by youre contenaunce ye be wondyr nyce,
You for to medyl with any retorucion.
To me ye haue sent a lettre of derusion,
Endyghted ful freshly with many coryous iclause.
Werfore I thank you as I fynde cause.

pryse = *worth, price*
fedyrfoy = *feverfew*

retorucion = *rhetorician*

coryous iclause = *curious*
(well made) phrases

The Ynglysch of Chaucere was nat in youre mynd,
Ne Tullyus termys wyth so gret elloquence,
But ye, as vncurts and crabbed of kynde,
Rolled hem on a hepe, it semyth by the sentence,
And so dare I boldly withoute ony offence
Answere to your letter, as fallyth to the purpose.
And thus I begynne, construe ye the glose.

Ynglysch of Chaucere =
Chaucer's English
Tullyus = Cicero's
vncurts = discourteous;
of kynde = by nature
sentence = meaning

construe ye the glose = understand
what I mean

Cryst of hys goodnesse and of hys gret myght
Formyd many a cryator to walke on the ground.
But he that beholdyth you by day and by nyght
Shal neuer haue cause in hert to be iocound.
Rememberyng your grete hede and your forhed round,
Wyth staryng eyen, visage large and huge,

cryator = creature

iocound = happy, jolly

And eyther of your pappys like a
water-bowge.

> pappys = breasts;
> bowge = bottle

Youre camusyd nose, with nosethryllys
brode,
Vnto the chyrch a noble instrument
To quenche tapers brennyng afore the roode,
Ys best apropred, at myne
avysament.
Your leud lokyng, doble of entent,
Wyth courtly loke, al of saferon hew,
That neuer wol fayle, the colour is so trew!

> camusyd = snubbed;
> nosethryllys = nostrils
>
> apropred = assigned; avysament = advice
>
> saferon = orange-yellow

Your babyr lyppys of colour ded and wan,
Wyth suche mouth lyke to Iacobys brother,
And yelow tethe not lyk to the swan,
Set wyde asondyr as yche cursed other.
In al a lond, who cowde fynde suche another,
Of alle feturys so vngodly for to se,
With brethe as swete as ys the elder tre.

> babyr = protruding
> Iacobys = Jacob's
> tethe = teeth
> asondyr = apart; as = as if
> a lond = the land
> feturys = features
> elder tre = elder tree (which stinks)

Youre body ys formyd al in proporcion,
With hangyng shuldres wauyng with euery wynde,
Smal in the bely as a wyn tonne,
Wyth froward fete, and crokyd bak behynde.
He that you wold haue alway in mynde,
And for your loue wold breke on oure reste,
I wold he were locched with Lucifer the
depeste.

> wyn tonne = wine tun
>
> locched = locked;
> depeste = deposed

And of youre atyre, shortly to devyse,
Your templers colured as the
lowcray,
With dagged hod, leyd on pancake
wyse,
Your bolwerkys, pectorellys, and al your
nyce aray.
Treuly me semyth ye ar a louely may!
And namely on halyday, whan ye tryp and daunce,
As a wilde goos kepyng your contenaunce!

> atyre = attire; devyse = describe
> templers = cloth headdress;
> lowcray = a kind of striped cloth?
> dagged hod = incised hood;
> wyse = like a . . .
> bolwerkys = breastworks (chest)
>
> may = maid

Adew, dere herte, for now I make an ende,
Vnto suche tyme that I haue better space.
The pyp and the pose to you I   *pyp and the pose = sickness and the cough*
    recomend,
And God of hys mercy graunte you so mykyl grace,
In Paradyse onys to haue a restyng place,   *onys = finally*
Vp by the nauel, fast by the   *nauel = navel; Vp . . . late =* Genesis 2.10–18,
    water gate,   with an ironic reference to Eve?
To loke after passage whan it cometh late.

Youre owne loue, trusty and trewe,
You haue forsake cause of a newe.   *cause = because*

VIII

Poems about Sex

The view of life which was developed in medieval scholastic philosophy argued that everything on earth had a purpose. This understanding was summed up by Thomas More in the sixteenth century when he remarked that God made flowers for their beauty, animals for their innocence, and men to serve Him wittily, in the tangle of their minds. Sex had an evident purpose too, but that was not the only reason that poets wrote about it. A Middle English poet often wrote about sex not only because the subject engaged him or her deeply, but also because he or she thought that (at least as a topic for poetry) it was funny. A well-known and early (twelfth-century) poem in a Cambridge University manuscript speaks, in a woman's voice, explaining that her lover is inadequate sexually, and does so in terms which are vigorously comic:

Atte ston castinges my lemman I ches,	*ston castinges = hurling competitions*
And atte wrastlinges sone I hym les;	*wrastlinges = wrestling; sone = soon*
Allas, that he so sone fel;	*fel = fell*
Wy nadde he stonde better, vile gorel?!*	*Wy = why; nadde = did he not; gorel = pig*

The poem (quoted from Cambridge University Library MS Ii.3.8 in the introduction to Robbins, p. xxxix) is not really about love on the athletic field, so much as it is about what happened (or didn't) in the bedroom. The triple pun on "stonde" needs no comment, and the one on "wrastlinges" only a moment's reflection (the man in question, a loser in every sense, was evidently himself "lost" to a third party). A contemporary sermon refers to the poem as a worthless dance song.

Yet the references to sex and to sexuality which such poems engage are often touched not only with humor, but also with a kind of innocence, as this one is, though often a studied innocence, and sometimes accompanied by guile. Whether from the narrator's point of view or the poet's, the action of making love, in certain poems at least, avoids moral censure, and delights in itself. Concerns with social implications, with family complications, with anything else at all, can be all but pushed aside – and this is particularly likely to be true when the point of view which is being represented is that of the man. In addition, these poems, as much as any others, delight in word play and in punning, and thus often manage to draw the reader into the intimate but lively world they have created.

Many modern readers rightly find these poems funny, though they also can be extravagant or intellectually engaging, and can help to remind us that this is the (at least implied) end of far more decorous poems, which apparently concern themselves only with love. In any event, while reading these poems we are not in the presence of prudes. So in order to understand them, first of all enjoy them.

37

Supplement 3899.3. British Library, London. MS Royal Appendix 58, fol. 5.
Davies no. 181. Duncan B no. 105. Robbins, p. xxxviii.

The "Western wind" cited in this brilliant little song is almost certainly
Zepherus, the spring rain recreating life which Chaucer invokes at the beginning of the *Canterbury Tales*, so whether the "small" rain of line 2 is "soft" or
"biting" (both readings are possible) must be determined by the way the reader
constructs the remainder of the poem. The lines are recorded in a Tudor song
book of the sixteenth century, but evidently antedate their manuscript. Another
song (*IMEV* 2953.5) from a different Tudor songbook (British Library MS Add.
5665, folio 69v) presents a very different image of a woman who does everything for her lover "to plese hym," but remains unsatisfied:

> O Blessed Lord how may this be,
> That Y am thus in hevynesse?   *hevynesse = sorrow, depression*
> And yet Y have do my besynesse   *do . . . besynesse = done my best*
> Ever to plese hym, with all my mygth,
> Bothe erly, late, by day and by nyghth.

Another poem (*IMEV* 1170), informally inserted in the sixteenth century into a
fifteenth-century manuscript, appears in British Library Royal MS 18 A vi, folio
22, and equally claims to take a woman's perspective, making it quite clear what
its author believes women want from men:

> He that wil be a lover in every wise,
> He muste have thre thingis whiche Jeame lackith:
> The first is goodlyhede at poynt devise;   *trans. = the first is perfect beauty*
> The secunde is manere, which manhoode makith;   *manere = manners*
> The thryd is goode, that no woman hatith.   *goode = wealth*
> Marke well this, that lovers wil be
> Muste nedys have oone of thes thre.

Individually, but also together, the three short poems included here record love's
incompleteness (or depression?), irony (or cynicism?), passion (or illusion?), and
taken together give a powerful sense of the range of voice and emotion present
in many Middle English secular love lyrics.

    The powerful short poem "Westron wynde" which follows below has been
examined by the notable American poet and novelist Robert Penn Warren, "Pure
and Impure Poetry," *Kenyon Review* 5 (1943): 228–54, and by Charles Frey, in
"Interpreting 'Western Wind,'" *ELH* 43 (1976): 259–78, and in "Transcribing and
Editing 'Western Wind,'" *Manuscripta* 23 (1979): 108–11. Its balladic associations

are noted by Boklund-Lagopoulou, *"I have a yong suster"* (2002). I cite the two poems printed above from Alexandra Barratt's fine anthology *Women's Writing in Middle English*, Longman's Annotated Texts (London and New York: Longman, 1992), p. 290, a book which lays to rest forever the old myth that late medieval Englishwomen couldn't or didn't write.

Westron wynde, when wyll thow blow,	*Westron = western*
The smalle rayne downe can rayne?	*smalle rayne = thin, soft rain*
Cryst, yf my love wer in my armys,	*yf = that; armys = arms*
And I yn my bed agayne!	

38

IMEV 194. Bodleian Library, Oxford. MS Rawlinson D. 913 (*SC* 13679), fol. 1v (j). Duncan A no. 10. Robbins no. 17.

Another of the Rawlinson lyrics, uniquely preserved on a strip of parchment, now bound into another manuscript, which contains, among other poems, "Maiden in the mor lay" (no. 20) and "Ich am of Irlaunde" (no. 22) (see figure 3, p. 75). It is usual to note the way in which the lyric presents a woman's name, but that name is almost certainly conventional, and the poem is most remarkable for its easy and immoral sophistication.

Burrow, in his study "Poems without Contexts: The Rawlinson Lyrics," (1984), pp. 1–26, suggests that the speaker is claiming to have spent the night with a woman whom, because there was an unnamed third party protecting her, he dared not carry off, and finds the poem both witty and cynical. Such a reading attaches a high degree of realism to the word "Darst," which may record nothing more than the speaker's conventional disinclination to remain with his beloved as dawn approaches in a kind of abbreviated *aubade* (in which a third party was often implied), but it does identify the poem's narrative context. The reading "Darst" in line 3 was one of those established by Peter Dronke in "The Rawlinson Lyrics," *Notes and Queries* 206 (1961): 245–6.

Al nist by the rose, Rose,	*nist = night*
Al nist by the rose I lay.	
Darst Ich noust the rose stele,	*Darst Ich noust = I dared not*
Ant yet I bar the flour awey.	*Ant = and*

39

IMEV 1299. British Library, London. MS Sloane 2593, fol. 10v. Davies no. 64.
Duncan A no. 122. Robbins no. 46.

See figure 2, p. 39. A well-known and very funny punning poem, whose voice may
have been influenced by one or more riddle poems, some of which were equally
uninhibited but more crude, of which these two may serve as examples: "I haue a
hole aboue my knee / And pricked yt was and pricked shal be. / And yet yt is not
sore / And yet yt shal be pricked more." (The answer proposed in the MS is: a
sheath for a knife.) Then there is this one: "Two stones hathe yt or els yt is wrong
/ With a bald hed and a tag somwhat long / & in the night when women lie
awake / Wit ther conscience they doe yt take." (The proposed answer is: a clock.)

The riddle poems are cited from Harry A. Peterson, ed., *Cambridge Middle English
Lyrics* (Seattle: University of Washington Press, 1962), nos 62 and 63, Cambridge
University Library MS Dd.5.76, fol. 1v. See also Lorrayne Y. Baird-Lange, "Symbolic Ambivalence in 'I haue a gentil cok,'" *Fifteenth-Century Studies* 11 (1985):
1–5. The poem is discussed in Boklund-Lagopoulou, "*I have a yong suster*" (2002).

I haue a gentil cok,	*gentil* = *noble; cok* = *cock* = MS reads *cook* throughout
Crowyt me ech day.	*ech* = MS omission
He doth me rysyn erly,	*rysyn* = *rise*
My matyins for to say.	*matyins* = *matins (prayers at dawn)*
I haue a gentil cok,	
Comyn he is of gret,	*gret* = *nobility*
His comb is of reed corel,	
His tayil is of get.	*get* = *jet (black)*
I haue a gentyl cok,	
Comyn he is of kynde,	*kynde* = pun: *nature, kin*
His comb is of red corel,	*corel* = MS *scorel* = *coral*
His tayl is of inde.	*inde* = *indigo*
His legges ben of asor,	*asor* = *azure*
So genitil and so smale,	*genitil* = *noble*
His spores arn of syluer qwyt,	*spores* = *back-claws; syluer qwyt* = *silver white*
Into the worte wale.	*worte wale* = *root of [his] spur*
His eynyn arn of cristal	*eynyn* = *eyes*
Lokyn al in aumbyr,	trans. = *looking like amber*
And euery nyght he perchit hym	
In myn ladyis chaumbyr.	

40

IMEV 1849. Gonville and Caius College, Cambridge. MS 383, page 41.
Davies no. 108. Duncan B no. 110. Greene no. 453. Robbins no. 28.

Unsurprisingly, perhaps, this carol is uniquely preserved, badly faded and inscribed in a tiny script, in a fifteenth-century exercise and commonplace notebook of a tri-lingual Oxford student, which also contains grammatical, theological, and legal notes and observations. It details, in a voice which is at once surprised, pained, and jocular, a seduction and its aftermath. A holy water clerk was a layman (the office was sometimes given to poor boys, particularly those intending to be clerics) whose responsibilities included such duties as assisting the priest at mass and sprinkling the congregation with holy water. The poem has been discussed (along with other texts) by Judith M. Bennett in Anne L. Klinck and Ann Marie Rasmussen, eds., *Medieval Woman's Song: A Cross-Cultural Approach* (2002), pp. 187–204, and by Neil Cartlidge, "'Alas, I go with Chylde': Representations of Extra-Marital Pregnancy in the Middle English Lyric," *English Studies* 5 (1998): 395–414.

Alas, alas the wyle,	
Thout Y on no gyle,	gyle = gile
So haue Y god chaunce,	trans. = as I may have good chance
Alas, alas the wyle,	
That euer I cowde daunce.	

Ladd Y the daunce	Ladd = led
A Myssomur Day,	
Y made smale trippus,	trippus = steps
Soth fore to say.	
Jak, oure haly-watur clerk,	clerk = MS clek = holy water clerk
Com be the way,	
And lokede me vpon,	
He thout that he was gay,	gay = good-looking, attractive
Thout Y on no gyle.	

Alas, alas . . .

Jak, oure haly-watur clerk,	
The yonge strippelyng,	
For the chesone of me	chesone = reason
He com to the ryng,	ryng = ring of dancers
And he trippede on my to,	to = toe

And made a twynkelyng,   *made a twynkelyng = gave a wink*
Euer he cam ner,
He sparet for nothynge.   *sparet = spared, held back (not at all)*
Thout Y on no gyle.

Alas, alas . . .

Jak, Ic wot, priyede   *priyede = looked closely*
In my fayre face,
He thout me ful werly,   *werly = fair*
So haue Y god grace,   *god = good*
As we turnden owre daunce   *turnden = turned*
In a narw place,   *narw = narrow*
Jak bed me the mouth,
A cussynge ther was.
Thout Y on no gyle.

Alas, alas . . .

Jak tho began
To rowne in myn ere: *rowne = whisper; ere = ear*
"Loke that thou be priuey
And grante that thou the bere,   *bere = keep secret*
A peyre wyht glouus   *peyre wyht glouus = pair of white gloves*
Ic ha to thyn were."   *ha = have*
"Gremercy, Iacke,"
That was myn answer.
Thout Y on no gyle.

Alas, alas . . .

Sone aftur euensong
Jak me mette:
"Com hom aftur thy glouus
That Ic the byhette."   *byhytte = promised*
Wan Ic to his chambur com,
Doun he me sette,
From hym mytte
Y nat go wan we were mette.   *we = MS omission*
Thout Y on no gyle.

Alas, alas . . .

Schetus and chalonus,   *Schetus and chalonus = sheets and blankets*
Ic wot, were yspredde,
Foresothe tho Jak and Ic
Wenten to bedde.
He prikede and he pransede,
Nolde he neuer lynne,   *lynne = ceased*
It was the murgust nyt   *murgust nyt = merriest night*
That euer Y cam ynne.
Thout Y on no gyle.

Alas, alas . . .

Wan Jak had don,
Tho he rong the belle,   *rong the belle = rang the bell (?)*
Al nyght ther
He made me to dwell,
Oft, I trewe, we haddum yserued   *trewe = know*
The reagged deuel of helle!   *reagged = MS reaggeth = shaggy*
Of othur smale burdus   *burdus = games*
Kep I nout to telle.   *kep = wish*
Thout I on no gyle.

Alas, alas . . .

The othur day at prime   *prime = prime, early morning*
Y com hom, as Ic wene,
Met Y my dame   *Met = MS meth; dame = mother*
Coppud and kene: *Coppud = bad tempered; kene = harsh*
"Sey, thou stronge strumpeth,   *stronge = bold*
Ware hastu bene?   *hastu = have you*
Thy trippyng and thy dauncyng
Wel it wol be sene!"   *trans. = will be well understood*
Thout Y on no gyle.

Alas, alas . . .

Euer bi on and bi on
My damme reched me clot,   *trans. = my mother beat me long*

Euer Y bar it preuey
Wyle that Y mouth,
Tyl my gurdul aros,
My wombe wax out,
"Euel yspunne yern
Euer it wole out."
Thout Y on no gyle.

Alas, alas . . .

bar it preuey = kept it secret
mouth = must
gurdul aros = belt stretched
wax = grew
trans. = *a bad tale, an evil-spun yarn*

IX

Ballads

Of all the genres which make up English and American poetry, ballads are among the best known and also, until very recently at least, the least studied. Their appeal is, and has been, pretty nearly universal: minstrels of old and modern folk singers alike have produced them in relatively large numbers, and though as a genre they are not easy to define, they are carefully preserved both in rare book rooms and in coffee houses, and are notable not only for their ability to draw their audience into the world which they create, but also in the way they linger in the imagination long after their performance (or their reading) is completed. Probably the most studied of these poems are those which are now called "traditional British ballads," though it is not possible to know when these separated off from other vernacular performance poems and came to constitute a separate sub-genre. Their early history is further complicated by the fact that the word *ballad*, derived from the French *ballade*, could be applied to virtually any form of sung narrative poetry, from "The Hunting of the Cheviot" to the longer Robin Hood narratives. But their lineage reaches down to Woodie Guthrie, Pete Seeger, Bob Dylan, and beyond.

As far as the traditional folk ballad is concerned, few examples are preserved in early medieval manuscripts (most British ballad manuscripts are sixteenth century or later), a circumstance which led to the speculation that most of them were in fact composed no earlier than the late eighteenth century, when the English antiquary Bishop Thomas Percy (1729–1811) published his three-volume collection *Reliques of Ancient English Poetry*, which first appeared in London in 1765. Percy had in fact compromised the edition by rewriting many of his texts so as to make them seem older than they appeared to be, a practice for which he was rightly taken to task by an irascible contemporary scholar, Joseph Ritson (1752–1803). The great modern collection of ballads was assembled by Harvard Professor Francis James Child (1825–96), whose *English and Scottish Popular Ballads* appeared in five volumes between 1882 and 1898. The ballads which follow below appear from Child's great anthology, with the numbers he assigned to them recorded throughout. Largely as the result of a relatively recent belief in the ballad's modern origin, their study has not flourished among medievalists, but there are reasons to think that this dismissal is in the process of being reversed, and that interest in these extraordinary poems is again beginning to engage students of medieval literature.

The Traditional Ballad

The traditional folk ballad is usually a narrative poem which seems almost to cultivate certain primitive "folk" characteristics. Often the text will begin *in medias res* ("in the middle of the thing"), or, as often, near the climax of the action. It will often lead up to a significant action, but may leap over other actions and details as it does so, often operating in the interest of suspense, sometimes doing so by employing a series of linked questions which add details and increase audience understanding by a kind of "incremental repetition." Usually the narrative voice in a ballad is quite impersonal and without emotion, even when recounting surprising, shocking or even horrific incidents.

One of the most important and also one of the earliest texts to give evidence of the narrative situations preserved in ballads is a Latin poem, "Foebus abierat" ("Phoebus had departed"), from about the year 1000. It combines both learned and popular sources in order to produce a lyric which already contains elements which would endure in the ballad tradition, and appear again in modern versions. I cite Peter Dronke's translation of the Latin text (he prints both in "Learned Lyric and Popular Ballad in the Early Middle Ages," *Studi Medievali* third series 17 (1976): 1–40):

> Phoebus had departed, his voyage past;
> his sister was riding with unbridled span,
> shedding her beams in forest springs,
> stirring wild creatures to prey, jaws agape.
> Mortals had let their limbs sink into sleep.
>
> One night in the April that has just gone by
> the image of my true-love stood before me;
> calling me softly, he touched me gently –
> his voice failed him, overcome by tears,
> he gave such sighs that he could not speak.
>
> At his touch I trembled fearfully;
> as if in terror I started up,

With outstretched arms I pressed my body to his,
and then I froze, utterly drained of blood –
for he had vanished! I was holding nothing!

Fully awake then, I called out loud:
"Where are you fleeing, I beg you, why so quickly?
Only wait, if you will – I too shall enter,
for I want to live with you forever!"
Soon I regretted having spoken so.

The windows of the terrace had been open,
the beams of Diana shone in all their beauty,
while I in my wretchedness grieved, ah so long.
Streams of tears flowed down over my cheeks;
till the next day my weeping never ceased.

Dronke points out that, in the Latin original, its meter is learned rather than popular, but that the poem as a whole represents a woman filled with medieval love-longing who suddenly and dramatically encounters the specter of her recently deceased lover. He indicates that most of the elements of the poem can be documented in the tradition of classical poetry (particularly that represented by Ovid), but the tone and the movement (not the emotion) of the poem seem to come clearly from the popular, what would become the balladic, tradition. The linking of death and love, the realization of horror, the opposition of nature and the grave, all of these, and more, would recur over the centuries. The most obvious links to this poem are those found in "The Unquiet Grave," a ballad whose medieval roots are well attested. But what is interesting too is the way other elements of the poem have entered into other and later ballads, including several which appear below, elements which you should consider and explore.

One particular interesting and reasonably early English ballad is "Saint Steven," *IMEV* 3058, preserved in only one fifteenth-century manuscript, MS Sloane 2593, folios 22v–23, a manuscript which has monastic associations at Bury St Edmunds, but which also contains, as already noted, many important Middle English lyrics. It is unusual to find a religious ballad as such, and Saint Steven, though attested to in *Acts of the Apostles* 6–7, is here represented as a "clerk" (= page?) who, entering the king's hall carrying the boar's head, responds to the Star of Bethlehem by announcing a conversion which, though supported by a traditional Christmas miracle, provokes his martyrdom. The narrative thus links his death (and so his feast day) to Christ's birth, which was and is traditional. The repetitions in the poem suggest song and even dance, and the distance between it and the carol is not great, but the poem does still adhere to the form of the traditional British ballad, and is thus usually accounted one of the earliest of its kind.

Saint Steuene was a clerk in Kyng Herowdis halle,
And seruyd hym of bred and cloth as every king befalle.   *as . . . befalle = happens to*

Steuyn out of kechoun cam with boris hed on honde,
He saw a sterre was fayr and bryght ouer Bedlem stonde.

He kyst adoun the bores hed and went into the hall,   *kyst = cast*
"I forsak the, King Herowdis, and thy werkes all."

"I forsake the, King Herowdis, and thy werkes all,
There is a chyld in Bedlem born is beter than we alle."

"Quat eylyt the, Steuene, quat is the befalle?   *eylyt = ails*
Lakkyt the eyther mete or drynk in King Herowdes halle?"   *Lakkyt = lack*

"Lakit me neyther mete ne drynk in King Herowdis hall,
Ther is a chyld in Bedlem born is beter than we alle."

"Quat eylyt the, Steuyn, art thou wod or thou   *wod = mad;*
    gynnyst to brede?   *gynnyst = go . . . wild*
Lakkyt the eythir gold or fe or ony ryche wede?"   *fe = fee, money; wede = garment*

"Lakyt me neyther gold ne fe ne non ryche wede,
Ther is a chyld in Bedlem born shal holpyn vs at our nede."

"That is also soth, Steuyn, also soth, I wys,   *also soth = as true*
As this capoun crowe shal that lyth here in myn dysh."   *capoun = chicken*

That word was not so sone seyd, that word in that halle,
The capon crew "*Christus natus est!*" among tho   Christus natus est! =
    lordes alle.   Christ is born!

"Rysyt vp myn turmentowres, be to and   *turmentowres = torturers;*
    al be on,   *be . . . on = all together*
And ledyt Steuyn out of this town and stonyt hym wyth ston."

Tokyn he Steuene and stonyd hym in the way,
And therfore is his euyn on Crystes owyn day.   *euyn = eve, feast day (26 December)*

The oral circulation of medieval and later ballads complicates the study of their medieval roots, and since much of their circulation took place well before the period in which most of them were written down, their study is best undertaken by referring, as far as possible, both to traditional and to more modern versions. That is why I have included more recent American examples of each of the traditional ballads I have printed below. In his largely bibliographical account of the ballad in *A Manual of the Writings in Middle English*, David C. Fowler points out that "scarcely more than a half dozen of the 305 Child ballads actually survive in a form earlier than the year 1500, and the majority of versions were collected in the nineteenth century" (VI, 1756). This putative circumstance has inhibited the discussion, among medievalists, of some important texts, and one of the central problems in ballad studies today is ascertaining which ballads may reasonably be called medieval, and how far certain others may. This issue has been engaged by Richard Firth Green and by Karin Boklund-Lagopoulou, see bibliographical note below, and who have set the study of medieval English ballads on a new course. In the five ballads which follow, for example, the last two, "The Unquiet Grave," and "The Three Ravens," have a clear claim to medieval origin. "Sir Patrick Spens" may possibly allude, if obliquely, to the drowning of many Scots nobles in 1281, as they were returning from having brought the Scottish king's daughter, Margaret, to her new husband, though evidence for the ballad as we have it first appears in Percy's *Reliques of Ancient English Poetry*, and Fowler thought (wrongly, in my opinion) that the ballad was, in its entirety, of relatively recent date.

An individual singer's skill, memory, and sense of tradition may testify to a ballad's longevity, even as its narrative echoes or encodes earlier versions. We need only reflect how many lyrics (not to speak of other vernacular compositions, from *Beowulf* to *Sir Gawain and the Green Knight*) reach us in only one medieval copy in order to see how many such popular texts, whose forms and whose numbers may well have been legion, we have almost certainly lost. Among these were probably "missing links" between earlier songs and preserved texts, including texts which the last two centuries have made widely familiar. "Barbara Allan" and in a different way "Lord Randal" contain medieval elements of betrayal, love-longing, suspense, and surprise integral to their composition, though they reach us in post-medieval forms and in versions which have undergone evident alteration. The very different narratives which each of these ballads records, for example, can be identified, changes having been made, in medieval Scandinavian ballads among others, one of which describes a man on his deathbed, dying because of a woman (D 318), another, a man who is warned by his mother that his betrothed has a new suitor, but does not believe her and is so poisoned when he visits the woman again (D 325). In each case the plot differs in the Middle English version, but the action is similar, and suggestive of medieval roots. It is sometimes said that in America the ballad changed direction, becoming more rational and less invested in the powerful themes of sex, death, and status which flourish in the European traditions. But these American versions (including the ones I have printed below) are impressive in their own way, and though they engage in the process of reinterpretation present in oral transmission generally, they also sought to reinvent balladic form in a way that is not yet fully understood.

Fowler, a great doubter in the antiquity of many ballads and a seeker of a kind of purity rarely available in great texts in any genre, thought that "Lord Randal" might "claim a certain antiquity by virtue of [its] European analogues" (VI, 1797), but thought it fallen from the status of a true medieval ballad, and unlikely to be earlier than the sixteenth century. On the contrary, in whatever form ballads have reached us, they represent the flowering of a medieval poetic tradition which was (and is) orally maintained, and whose parameters, themes, and accomplishments are only now beginning to come clear, as scholars turn again to their origins (as far as these can be fairly determined) and to the nature and circumstances of their circulation.

The Modern Ballad

Still, even with what continuity there has been, it is worth remembering that balladic practice differed from age to age, from balladeer to balladeer, and that its development is far from complete. Though traditional ballads like those I have been referring to differ from the productions of contemporary and near-contemporary balladeers like Woodie Guthrie (1912–67) or Pete Seeger (b. 1919), Bob Dylan or Joan Baez (both b. 1941), there are similarities as well, even with these most modern of singers. Probably the contrast between Guthrie and Seeger is the most instructive. Guthrie, the son of a father who failed financially and of a mother who suffered from a hereditary nervous disorder, Huntington's chorea, which would in time destroy her son, kept a hard edge on his ballads. It was this that Bob Dylan admired and emulated during his relatively brief period of social activism (memorialized in his albums *The Freewheelin' Bob Dylan* and *The Times They Are A-Changing* (both 1963)), and that Joan Baez captured, in a resonant if personal way, in "Diamonds and Rust." Woodie Guthrie's most famous song, "This Land is Your Land," is not as pointed as his most powerful lyrics; more revealing is the sign he kept on his guitar: "This machine kills fascists." His close friend Pete Seeger, middle class and Harvard educated, warmly shared (and in the 1950s suffered from) Guthrie's 1930s socialism, but was more consistently (though often subtly) political in his compositions, especially in what became his most popular songs, "Where Have All the Flowers Gone?," "Turn, Turn, Turn," and "If I Had a Hammer." The making of ballads, like the making of lyrics, is far from over, and ballads, like lyrics, are far from dead.

But like his predecessors, Dylan also owed a very direct debt to the ballad tradition, and it is particularly evident in his best protest songs. "Blowin' in the Wind," which David Hajdu has somewhat condescendingly described as "a pretty and memorable, if repetitive, adaptation of the traditional antislavery ballad 'No More Auction Block'" (p. 117), uses the ballad's burden or refrain as effectively as any modern song. And although the questions which "A Hard Rain's a-Gonna Fall," seeks to address are those echoed in the traditional English ballad "Lord Randal" (no. 43, below), the song's lyrics, among the best in Dylan's canon, seem to have begun as a poetic response to the nuclear war which the Cuban Missile Crisis seemed to presage, but then to have been transformed into a song with far-reaching social implications. It gains its power and effect by brilliantly contrasting the impersonal questions and descriptions found in ballads like "Lord Randal" with the evident horror of the poem's apocalyptic imagery ("I met a young woman whose body was burning"), a horror which a nuclear winter – or any like apocalypse – would inescapably bring about. Thus the lyric raises, if not entirely directly since some of its imagery is cosmic and natural, social and political issues toward which the traditional ballad is usually indifferent. In his best protest songs Dylan reformulates the restraint and even formality of the traditional ballad by adapting its suspense and surprise to a larger social or political purpose.

Taken together, modern ballads develop social themes only indirectly present, if present at all, in traditional ballads, since traditional ballads usually avoid attaching the distress they record to historical persons or events, and maintain a degree of impersonality which generally separates them from their modern counterparts. But both engage the audience in a story which, by verbal repetition and narrative extremity, impels sympathy, and which often ends badly. In traditional ballads social class is often hinted at, not foregrounded; but it is present. Death and failure reflect personal striving and sometimes social disappointment, and these realities matter more than political effect. The modern tradition is invested in them as well, albeit, for the most part, as effects, not causes.

There may seem to be an exception to the ahistorical character of traditional ballads in the fact that by the fourteenth century (not before) poems concerning Robin Hood appear, but, as Stephen Knight has argued in *Robin Hood: A Complete Study of the English Outlaw* (1994), there is no really compelling evidence that the famous outlaw ever existed, and his presence may hint at a political strain in medieval ballads, one which anticipates more modern songs. The old idea that ballads emerged "from the folk" is increasingly difficult to sustain, and in cases where the names of their makers are known, quite impossible. But whatever their origin, many ballads were obviously composed by excellent singers, who created them at least in part because they knew their tradition and found freedom and power in its conventions. The perhaps predictable result of this circumstance was that numerous versions of the more familiar ballads circulated widely, both in Britain and America.

The Ballad in the Modern World

The American versions of traditional British ballads which I have printed below were collected by the great American balladeer and student of American folk music John Jacob Niles (1892–1980), in Appalachia, primarily during the 1930s. The circumstances of their transmission before they reached Niles are obscure, though their sources are not, and by way of illustration I have noted which ballads are also recorded in the *Frank G. Brown Collection of North Carolina Folklore* ("*Brown Collection*"), and in the *Ozark Folksongs* edited by Vance Randolph ("Randolph"), cited in my Abbreviations, above. Collectively, these versions lend further support to the theory that many ballads often described confidently as "Tudor or Stewart" are in fact considerably older, and richly deserve a place in any anthology of medieval lyrics and songs. In many cases, the ballads Niles collected had not been published previously, or even written down, before he found them. In the late medieval period, how much more true must this have been of ballads which, lacking the literary character of carols, and the need of carols for several identical texts, were orally transmitted from one balladeer to the next, many of them making additions or alterations, major or minor, until after a period they appeared in print, like a fly in amber.

John Jacob Niles was a man of evident cultivation (his preferred instrument was the dulcimer), and in the "Postscript" to his *Ballad Book* he recounts some remarks made to him by an unnamed instructor when he was a student of Greek Drama at the University of Lyon, which he recalled as being that "starkest tragedy and the most bombastic, slapstick comedy are the most likely to remain in the current of human consciousness. They are quite sure to be republished as books, attended as plays, and revered as music." For Niles, this helped to explain why so many traditional ballads, including 39 of the traditional Child ballads he had printed, were as thematically tragic as they were. Thus it is that traditional ballads narrate a simple, often painful, story, both impersonally and directly, but in a way which lends itself to oral transmission, and so focus on action, dialogue, and verbal repetition. As noted, they tend to be both highly individual, often identifying a named but not historical person in a moment of extreme distress; and also universal, regularly engaging such themes as loss, death, and (less often) love, which they reveal with few details, beginning *in medias res*, and jumping from scene to scene with little in the way of transition. Their accompanying music aids greatly in their survival, and is the reason that, thanks to their singers' inventiveness, they exist in as many versions as they do. But even these relatively simple rules are subject to modification and revision, and having read both these and more modern examples too, you should not hesitate to compose your own, as John Jacob Niles did.

All of the ballads I have printed below both exist and have existed in many versions, not just three or four. I cannot print them all here, though a good deal more can be found in Child, but I have printed two early versions before the recent one in the hope of showing some at least of the variations which balladeers employ. The oral character of the changes they introduced will be apparent when you compare the details within the texts. Notice how easy most of the narratives are to add to, how easily details lend themselves to elaboration (or to cutting). Thus, none of these is a "set text." They are all in flux; they are all in play.

Bibliographical Note

For the association of music with these ballads see Bertrand Harris Bronson, *The Traditional Tunes of the Child Ballads with Their Texts, According to the Extant Records of Great Britain and America.* 4 volumes (Princeton: Princeton University Press, 1959–72), and Bronson's *The Ballad as Song* (Berkeley and Los Angeles: University of California Press, 1969), especially "The Interdependence of Ballad Tunes and Texts," pp. 37–63, and "Habits of the Ballads as Song," pp. 92–111. Niles' *Ballad Book* is cited under Abbreviations, above, but it should be noted too that Niles' own extensive archives are preserved in the John Jacob Niles Center for American Music at the Fine Arts Library of the University of Kentucky. There were numerous recordings made of Niles' own performances, of which "John Jacob Niles' 50th Anniversary Album" (RCA Camden CAL 330), and "John Jacob Niles Sings American Folksongs" (RCA Camden CAL 245), were probably the best known.

Peter Dronke's important study which I have cited is "Learned Lyric and Popular Ballad in the Early Middle Ages," *Studi Medievali* third series 17 (1976): 1–40, reprinted in his *The Medieval Poet and his World*, Storia e Letteratura 164 (Rome: Edizioni di Storia e Letteratura, 1984), pp. 167–207. Dronke's edition of the Latin text appears in *Medieval Latin and the Rise of European Love-Lyric*, second edition (Oxford: Clarendon Press, 1968), II, 334–41, where he reasonably calls it "one of the most remarkable texts in Medieval Latin" (p. 337). There is a particularly good account of the state of ballad studies today, together with an excellent study of some of the oral characteristics in traditional ballads and a discussion of the ways in which they may preserve traces, if not more, of their medieval past, in Richard Firth Green, "The Ballad and the Middle Ages," in Helen Cooper and Sally Mapstone, eds., *The Long Fifteenth Century: Essays for Douglas Gray* (Oxford: Clarendon Press, 1997), pp. 163–84. Green's defense is further supported by Boklund-Lagopoulou, "*I have a yong suster*" (2002), who is particularly concerned with historical and comic ballads, and with their connections to popular song, and has discussed individually most of the texts printed below.

See too Thomas J. Garbáty, "Rhyme, Romance, Ballad, Burlesque, and the Confluence of Form," in Robert F. Yeager, ed., *Fifteenth-Century Studies: Recent Essays* (Hamden,

Conn.: Archon Books for the Shoe String Press, 1984), pp. 283–301; and Douglas Gray, "Medieval English Ballads," in Patricia Shaw, et al., eds. *Actas del Primer Congreso Internacional de la Sociedad Española de Lengua y Literatura Inglesa Medieval* (Oviedo, 1989), 129–54. Tristram Potter Coffin, *The British Traditional Ballad in North America*, revised edition 1977, cited above, is an essential beginning point for these texts; still useful too is MacEdward Leach and Tristram P. Coffin, eds., *The Critics and the Ballad* (Carbondale, Ill.: University of Illinois Press, 1961, rpt. 1973), and the entry "Ballads" by David C. Fowler in volume 6 of Albert E. Hartung, ed., *A Manual of the Writings in Middle English, 1050–1500* (New Haven: Connecticut Academy of Arts and Sciences, 1980), 1753–1808, and 2019–70. Fowler has defended his late dating for many of the lyrics in his *Literary History of the Popular Ballad* (Durham, N. C.: Duke University Press, 1968).

The Scandinavian ballads referred to above are listed and recorded in Bengt R. Jonsson, Svale Solheim, and Eva Danielson, eds., *The Types of the Scandinavian Medieval Ballad: A Descriptive Catalogue*, The Institute for Comparative Research in Human Culture, Oslo, Series B, LIX (Oslo, Bergen and Tromsø: Universitetsforlaget, 1978), D 318, D 325. For the transition to the modern ballad see Natascha Wuerzbach, *The Rise of the Street Ballad, 1550–1650*, trans. Gayna Walls, European Studies in English Literature (Cambridge: Cambridge University Press, 1990), and an interesting study involving American transmission of traditional British ballads by William B. McCarthy, "The Americanization of Scottish Ballads: Counter-evidence from the Southwest of Scotland," in Joseph Harris, ed., *The Ballad and Oral Literature*, Harvard English Studies 17 (Cambridge, Mass. and London: Harvard University Press, 1991), pp. 97–108. For the Robin Hood ballads and songs see R. B. Dobson and J. Taylor, *Rymes of Robin Hood: An Introduction to the English Outlaw* (London: William Heinemann, and Pittsburgh: University of Pittsburgh Press, 1976), and now in particular, Stephen Knight, *Robin Hood: A Complete Study of the English Outlaw* (Oxford: Blackwell, 1994). There is a short survey of post-medieval ballads in British literature, G. Malcolm Laws, Jr., *The British Literary Ballad: A Study in Poetic Imitation* (Carbondale and Edwardsville: Southern Illinois University Press, 1972). For the more contemporary ballads I have touched upon above, I am indebted to Michael Gray, *Song and Dance Man III: The Art of Bob Dylan* (London and New York: Cassell, 2000); to David Hajdu, *Positively 4th Street: The Lives and Times of Joan Baez, Bob Dylan, Mimi Baez Farina and Richard Farina* (New York: North Point Press, 2001); and to Clinton Heylin, *Bob Dylan: Behind the Shades Revisited* (New York: William Morrow for HarperCollins Publishers, 2000). Many studies of Dylan verge on hagiography; Hajdu's and Heylin's do no such thing, but perhaps have difficulty separating his celebrity, and what they represent as his narcissism, from his art. For a sympathetic but not uncritical account of Dylan see Howard Sounes, *Down the Highway: A Life of Bob Dylan* (New York: Grove Press, 2001).

41

Sir Patrick Spens

Child no. 58. *Brown Collection* no. 16. Coffin no. 58.

Bishop Percy's *Reliques of Ancient English Poetry* (London, 1765) I, 71, announces that the version printed is: "given from two MS Copies, transmitted from Scotland." But Percy himself may well have taken a hand in producing the text which he printed.

Thus, this is one of those ballads suspected of being an eighteenth-century "forgery," though whatever form in took in 1765, it is certainly possible that it began life earlier, in a version yet to be identified. It remains one of the most famous of all English ballads, and one argument for a relatively early date of composition (or at least invention) rests upon the suggestion that its earliest version may have contained a memory of the drowning, in 1281, of many Scots nobles who were returning from escorting Margaret, the daughter of the Scottish king, and her new husband Eric of Norway, to their new home. Still, "Sir Patrick Spens" himself clearly lies outside of the historical record, and is almost certainly a balladic invention – though not necessarily Percy's. In time, the ballad traveled to the Americas, and in 1934 the great balladeer and student of ballads John Jacob Niles recorded a version sung by a Mr Christopher Bell (b. 1849) who had fought as a Confederate soldier in the American Civil War, and subsequently made his living by teaching and singing ballads. The American version follows the English versions, below.

Sir Patrick Spens

Child 58 A

The king sits in Dumferling toune,	*Dumferling = modern Dunfermline, a favorite residence, and burial place, of the Scottish kings*
Drinking the blude-reid wine.	*blude-reid = blood red*
"O whar will I get guid sailor,	*guid = good*
To sail this schip of mine?"	

Up and spak an eldern knicht,
Sat at the king's richt kne:

"Sir Patrick Spence is the best sailor,
That sails upon the se."

The king has written a braid letter,   *braid = broad, public*
And signd it wi his hand,
And sent it to Sir Patrick Spence,
Was walking on the sand.

The first line that Sir Patrick red,
A loud lauch lauched he.   *lauch = laugh*
The next line that Sir Patrick red,
The teir blinded his ee.   *teir = tear; ee = eye*

"O wha is this has don this deid,   *wha = who; deid = deed*
This ill deid don to me,
To send me out this time o' the yeir,
To sail upon the se?

"Mak hast, mak haste, my mirry men all,
Our guid schip sails the morne."
"O say na sae, my master deir,   *na sae = not so; deir = dear*
For I feir a deadlie storme.

"Late late yestreen I saw the new moone   *yestereen = last evening*
Wi the auld moone in hir arme.   *auld = old*
And I feir, I feir, my deir master,
That we will cum to harme."

O our Scots nobles wer richt laith   *laith = reluctant*
To weet their cork-heild schoone.   *schoone = shoes*
But lang owre a' the play wer playd,   *owre a' = before all*
Thair hats they swam aboone.   *aboone = above*

O lang, lang, may their ladies sit,
Wi thair fans into their hand,
Or eir they se Sir Patrick Spence   *Or eir = before*
Cum sailing to the land.

O lang, lang, may the ladies stand,
Wi their gold kems in their hair,   *kems = combs*
Waiting for thair ain deir lords,   *ain = own*
For they'll se tham na mair.   *na mair = no more*

Haf owre, haf owre to Aberdour,
It's fiftie fadom deip,   *fadom = fathoms*
And thair lies Sir Patrick Spence,
Wi the Scots lords at his feit.   *feit = feet*

Child 58 D

The king sits in Dumferling town,
Drinking the blood red wine:
"O where will I get a good skipper
To sail seven ships o mine?"
O Where will, etc.

O up then spake a bra young man,
And a bra young man was he,   *bra = brave, excellent, here with irony*
"Sir Andrew Wood is the best skipper
That ever saild the sea."

The king has written a bra letter,   *bra = broad*
And seald it wi his hand,   *wi = with*
And ordered Sir Andrew Wood
To come at his command.

"O wha is this or wha is that,   *wha = what, who*
Has tauld the king o me?   *o = of*
For had he been a better man,
He might ha tauld a lee."   *tauld a lee = told a lie*

***

As I came in by the Inch, Inch, Inch,
I herd an auld man weep: *auld = old*
"Sir Andrew Wood and a' his men   *a' = all*
Are drowned in the deep."

O lang, lang may yon ladies stand   *lang = long*
Their fans into their hands,   *into = in*
Before they see Sir Andrew Wood
Come sailing to dry land.

O laith laith were our Scottish   *laith = loath, unwilling*
T weit their cork-heeld shoon;

But ere that a' the play was plaid
They wat their heads aboon.   *wat = wet; aboon = above*

Nore-east, nore-west frae Aberdeen   *frae = from*
Is fifty fathom deep,
And there lies good Sir Andrew Wood,
And a' the Scottish fleet.

Well-known ballads could in time produce not so much other versions as progeny:

Child 58 L

Our ship it was a gudely ship,
Its topmast was of gold,
And at every tack of needlework
There hung a silver bell.

Up started the mermaid by our ship,
Wi the glass and the comb in her hand: *glass = mirror*
"Reek about, reek about, my merry men,   *Reek = turn*
Ye are not far from land."

"You lie, you lie, you pretty mermaid,
Sae loud as I hear you lie;   *Sae = so*
For since I have seen your face this nicht,   *nicht = night*
The land I will never see."

We had na sailed a league but ane,   *na = not; ane = one*
A league but barely three,
Till all we and our goodly ship
Was all drowned in the sea.

Lang, lang may our ladies stand,
Wi their seams into their hand,
Looking for Sir Patrick's ship,
That will never come to land.

Patrick Spencer

American version (1934), *Ballad Book*, p. 135.

Oh, the King stood with his fighting men,
The King sat in his court.
A sailor man he sore did need,
And one of good report, report,
And one of good report.

Then went the King to Dunfertown
To burble the wine so red,
"Are all my sailing captains gone?
Mayhap they all be dead."
(*Repeat last two lines of each stanza.*)

"The season's off," an old knight said.
"'Tis winter," cried a youth.
"Your cargo and your ship will drown
In the Northern Sea, forsooth."

Oh, strong was Patrick Spencer's arm
And sharp his seaman's eye,
And sharper still the sense of him
To ken a sullen sea.

The King spoke to his footy page,
"Ye must not stop nor stay
Until Pat Spencer well doth know
The royal will today."

"What man hath done me all this ill,
What man hath done me sore,
To send me forth agin the sea
When I should not sail more?

"Oh, hasten ships and sailor men,
Oh, hasten sandlers, too,   *sandlers = chandlers?* (Niles' note)
Oh, hasten down the endless sea
The King's wild will to do.

"For two days past I saw the sun
And yester eve'ing the moon,
Tonight I saw a blood-red star
And know my end is soon."

When Patrick Spencer sailed away,
A laugh did light his eye.
When Patrick Spencer came to rest,
Hit was his time to die.

Oh, some sit in the chimney book,   *book* = *nook* (Niles' note)
And some walk on the strand,
And some do watch the whole day out
For Spencer's ship to land.

But Patrick Spencer's long since home
Where sailors all must haven.
The Scottish lords and all their crew
Are in the sailors' heaven.

Oh, at his feet the Scottish lords
Lay mid the ocean's wailing,
And at his head, in letters red,
The orders for his sailing.

42

Bonnie Barbara Allan

Child no. 84. *Brown Collection* no. 27. Coffin no. 84. Randolph no. 21.

A ballad about love and rejection, death followed by sorrow and subsequent death, this English ballad became a favorite in the United States. Although in a later Child version (84 B) the death-bell seems to ring "Unworthy Barbara Allen," it is possible to believe that the cause cited here masks a more complex social attitude, perhaps one associated with class. Niles located (and prints on p. 205) a "complete" American text, but I have printed instead one which shows variation and innovation, which are at the heart of the balladeer's art.

Bonnie Barbara Allan

Child 84 A

It was in and about the Martinmas time,
When the green leaves were a falling,
That Sir John Graeme, in the West Country,
Fell in love with Barbara Allan.

He sent his men down through the town,
To the place where she was dwelling.
"O haste and come to my master dear,
Gin ye be Barbara Allan."

O hooly, hooly rose she up,   *hooly = slowly*
To the place where he was lying,
And when she drew the curtain by,
"Young man, I think you're dying."

"O it's I'm sick, and very, very sick,
And 't is a' for Barbara Allan."
"O the better for me ye's never be,
Tho your heart's blood were a spilling.

"O dinna ye mind, young man," said she,   *dinna = did not*
"When ye was in the tavern a drinking,

That ye made the healths gae round and round,   *gae = go*
And slighted Barbara Allan?"

He turned his face unto the wall,
And death was with him dealing,
"Adieu, adieu, my dear friends all,
And be kind to Barbara Allan."

And slowly, slowly, raise she up,
And slowly, slowly, left him,
And sighing said, she could not stay,
Since death of life had reft him.   *reft = bereft, deprived*

She had not gane a mile but twa,   *gane = gone; but twa = or two*
When she heard the death-bell ringing,
And every jow that the death-bell geid,   *jow = toll, ring; geid = gave*
It cry'd "Woe to Barbara Allan."

"O Mother, Mother, make my bed,
O make it saft and narrow,   *saft = soft*
Since my love died for me today,
I'll die for him tomorrow."

Child 84 B

In Scarlet Town, where I was bound,
There was a fair maid dwelling,
Whom I had chosen to be my own,
And her name it was Barbara Allen.

All in the merry month of May,
When green leaves they were springing,
This young man on his death-bed lay,
For the love of Barbara Allen.

He sent his man unto her then,
To the town where she was dwelling,
"You must come to my master dear,
If your name be Barbara Allen.

"For death is printed in his face,
And sorrow's in him dwelling,
And you must come to my master dear,
If your name be Barbara Allen."

"If death be printed in his face,
And sorrow's in him dwelling,
Then little better shall he be,
For bonnie Barbara Allen."

So slowly, slowly she got up,
And so slowly she came to him,
And all she said when she came there,
"Young man, I think you're dying."

He turned his face unto her then,
"If you be Barbara Allen,
My dear," said he, "come pity me,
As on my death-bed I am lying."

"If on your death-bed you be lying,
What is that to Barbara Allen?
I cannot keep you from [your] death,
So farewell," said Barbara Allen.

He turned his face unto the wall
And death came creeping to him:
"Then adieu, adieu, and adieu to all,
And adieu to Barbara Allen."

And as she was walking on a day,
She heard the bells a ringing,
And it did seem to ring to her
"Unworthy Barbara Allen."

She turned herself round about,
And she spy'd the corps a coming:
"Lay down, lay down the corps of clay,
That I may look upon him."

And all the while she looked on,
So loudly she lay laughing,
While all her friends cry'd [out] amain,
"Unworthy Barbara Allen!"

When he was dead, and laid in grave,
Then death came creeping to she,
"O mother, mother make my bed,
For his death hath quite undone me.

"A hard-hearted creature that I was,
To slight one that loved me so dearly,
I wish I had been more kinder to him,
The time of his life when he was near me."

So this maid she then did die,
And desired to be buried by him,
And repented her self before she dy'd,
That ever she did deny him.

Barbara Allen

American version (1934), *Ballad Book*, p. 206

Early, early in the spring
The spring buds they were swelling,
Sweet William Gay on his deathbed lay
For the love of Barbara Allen.

He sent his servant to her tower,
He sent him there a-dwelling,
Said, "Young maiden there's a call for you,
If your name be Barbara Allen."

Slowly, slowly she got up
And slowly she went to him.
And all she said when she got there was,
"Young man, I think you're dying."

"Oh yes I'm sick, and I'm very sick
And death is with me dwelling,
And never no better shall ever I be
Till I get Barbara Allen."

"Oh yes you're sick, and you're very sick,
And death is with you dwelling,
And never no better shall ever you be
For you can't get Barbara Allen."

Slowly, slowly she got up
And slowly she went from him.
She had not got a mile in town
When she heard the death bells tolling.

She looked to the east, she looked to the west,
She saw his cold corpse coming.
"Hand down, hand down that corpse of clay,
That I may gaze upon him."

First she wept and then she mourn
And then she burst out crying.
"I might have saved that young man's life
If I had done my duty.

"Oh Mama, oh Mama, go make my bed,
Go make it long and narrow,
Sweet William Gay died for me today,
I die for him tomorrow.

"Oh Papa, oh Papa, go dig my grave,
Go dig it long and narrow.
Sweet William died in love for me,
I'll die for him in sorrow."

Sweet William died on Saturday,
Barbara died on Sunday,
Their mothers died for love of both,
They died the following Monday.

They buried Sweet William in one church yard,
And Barbara in the other.
From William's grave sprang a red, red rose,
From Barbara's grave a briar.

They grew and they grew up the old church's tower,
Till they could not grow higher.
And they looped and they tied a true love's knot,
The rose around the briar.

43

Lord Randal

Child no. 12. *Brown Collection* no. 6. Coffin no. 12. Randolph no. 5.

One of the most popular ballads anywhere (Child notes 19 versions), and though its origin is obscure, Sir Walter Scott believed that it could be traced to the death of Thomas Randolph, nephew of Robert Bruce, who died, poisoned by an English priest, in 1332. Another account suggests that the ballad may possibly allude to the nephew of Ranulf or Randal III, sixth Earl of Chester, who died in 1232, whose wife is said to have tried to poison him. Many modern scholars consider that any historical background must be largely, if not entirely, conjectural.

It proved, however, to be extraordinarily popular in America under a variety of titles, being known often as "Jimmy Randal," and, in a Southern Michigan version in which the protagonist bequeaths to his murderer "the great keys of hell," as "A Cup of Cold Poison." John Jacob Niles located 52 American versions, 40 of which mentioned poisoning by eels, which were usually said to have been fried. The American version printed below Niles collected from Solomon and Beth Holcolm in Whitesburg, Kentucky, on July 8, 1932. The Michigan version is printed in Emelyn Elizabeth Gardner and Geraldine Jencks Chickering, eds., *Ballads and Songs of Southern Michigan* (Hatboro, Penn.: Folklore Associates, 1967), pp. 35–6.

Lord Randal

Child 12 A

"O where ha you been, Lord Randal, my son?
And where ha you ben, my handsome young man?"
"I ha been at the greenwood; Mother, mak my bed soon,
For I'm wearied wi hunting, and fain wad lie down."

"An wha met ye there, Lord Randal, my son,
An what met you there, my handsome young man?"
"O I met wi my true-love; Mother, mak my bed soon,
For I'm wearied wi huntin, and fain wad lie down."

"And what did she give you, Lord Randal, my son.
And what did she give you my handsome young man?"
"Eels fried in a pan; Mother, mak my bed soon,
For I'm wearied wi hunting and fain wad lie down."

"And wha gat your leavins, Lord Randal, my son,
And wha gat your leavins, my handsome young man?"
"My hawks and my hounds; Mother, mak my bed soon,
For I'm wearied wi hunting and fain wad lie down."

"And what becam of them, Lord Randal, my son,
And what becam of them, my handsome young man?"
"They stretched their legs out an died; Mother, mak my bed soon,
For I'm wearied wi hunting and fain wad lie down."

"O I fear you are poisoned, Lord Randal, my son,
O I fear you are poisoned, my handsome young man."
"O yes, I am poisoned; Mother, mak my bed soon,
For I'm sick at heart, and fain wad lie down."

"What d'ye leave to your mother, Lord Randal, my son,
What d'ye leave to your mother, my handsome young man?"
"Four and twenty milk kye; Mother, mak my bed soon,   *kye = cows*
For I'm sick at the heart, and I soon wad lie down."

"What d'ye leave to your sister, Lord Randal, my son,
What d'ye leave to your sister, my handsome young man?"
My gold and my silver; Mother, mak my bed soon,
For I'm sick at heart, and fain wad lie down."

"What d'ye leave to your brother, Lord Randal, my son,
What d'ye leave to your brother, my handsome young man?"
"My horses and my lands: Mother, mak my bed soon,
For I'm sick of heart, and fain wad lie down."

"What d'ye leave to your true-love, Lord Randal, my son,
What d'ye leave to your true-love, my handsome young man?"
"I leave her hell and fire; Mother, mak my bed soon,
For I'm sick at the heart and I fain wad lie down."

This ballad lent itself easily both to concision as well as to addition, according to the balladeer's need, art or whim. Note the simple repetition of lines without the variation of other versions, and the elimination (as already understood) both of the protagonist's bequests, and the charge of murder at the end.

Child 12 E

"Ah where have you been, Lairde Rowlande, my son?
Ah where have you been, Lairde Rowlande, my son?"
"I've been to the wild woods; Mither, mak my bed soon,
For I'm weary wi hunting, and faine would lie down."

"Oh you've been at your true love's, Lairde Rowlande, my son!
Oh you've been at your true love's, Lairde Rowlande, my son!"
"I've been at my true love's; Mither, mak my bed soon,
For I'm weary wi hunting, and faine would lie down."

"What got you to dinner, Lairde Rowlande, my son?
What got you to dinner, Lairde Rowlande, my son?"
"I got eels boild in brue; Mither, mak my bed soon,
For I'm weary wi hunting and faine would lie down."

"What's become of your warden, Lairde Rowlande, my son?
What's become of your warden, Lairde Rowlande, my son?"
"He died in the muirlands; Mither, mak my bed soon,
For I'm weary wi hunting, and faine would lie down."

"What's become of your stag-hounds, Lairde Rowlande, my son?
What's become of your stag-hounds, Lairde Rowlande, my son?"
"They swelled and they died; Mither, mak my bed soon,
For I'm weary wi hunting, and faine would lie down."

Child 12 L

"Whar hae ye been a' the day, Willie doo, Willie doo?   *doo = dear*
Whar hae ye been a' the day, Willie, my doo?"

"I've been to see my step-mother; make my bed, lay me down;
Make my bed, lay me down, die I shall now."

"What got ye frae your step-mother, Willie doo, Willie doo?   *frae = from*
What got ye frae your step mother, Willie, my doo?"

"She gae me a speckled trout; make my bed, lay me down;
She gae me a speckled trout, die shall I now."

"Whar got she the speckled trout, Willie doo, Willie doo?"
"She got it amang the heather hills; die shall I now."

"What did she boil it in, Willie doo, Willie doo?"
"She boiled it in the billie-pot; die shall I now."

"What gaed she you for to drink, Willie doo, Willie doo?
What gaed she you for to drink, Willie my doo?"

"She gaed me hemlock stocks: make my bed, lay me down;
Made in the brewing pot; die I shall now."

They made his bed, laid him down, poor Willie doo, Willie doo;
He turned his face to the wa; he's dead now.   *wa = wall*

Jimmy Randal

American version (1932), *Ballad Book*, p. 59

"Oh where have you been, Jimmy Randal, my son,
Oh where have you rovèd, my oldest dear one?"
"Oh Mither, oh Mither, go make my bed soon,
'Cause my courtin' has sicked me and I fain would lay doon."

"What had you for supper, Jimmy Randal, my son,
What had you for supper, my oldest dear one?"
"Some fried eels and parsnips, go make my bed soon,
'Cause my courtin' has sicked me and I fain would lie doon."

"What will you give me, Jimmy Randal, my son,
What will you your mother, my oldest dear one?"
"My house and my lands, Mither, make my bed soon,
'Cause my courtin' has sicked me and I fain would lie doon."

"What will you your father, Jimmy Randal, my son,
What will you your father, my oldest dear one?"
"My wagon and team, Mither, make my bed soon,
'Cause my courtin' has sicked me and I fain would lie doon."

"What will you your brother, Jimmy Randal my son,
What will you your brother, my oldest dear one?"
"My horn and my hound, Mither, make my bed soon,
'Cause my courtin' has sicked me and I fain would lie doon."

"What will you your sweetheart, Jimmy Randal my son,
What will you your sweetheart, my oldest dear one?"
"Bullrushes, bullrushes, and them all parched brown,
'Cause she gave me the pizen that I did drink down."

"And when you are dead, Jimmy Randal my son,
And when you are dead, my oldest dear one?"
"Go dig me a grave 'side my grandfather's son,
'Cause my courtin' has sicked me and I fain would lie down."

44

The Unquiet Grave

Child no. 78. *Brown Collection* no. 24. Coffin no. 78.

The antiquity of this ballad, in which a grieving lover is warned by his long-dead lover to cease lamenting her and seeking a final kiss or he will die as well, is a matter of dispute, though it may well include a balladic reconstruction of a more ancient text, and few doubt that it antedates Child's nineteenth-century versions. Niles located ten American versions, including one he collected from Corie Netter at Flat Lick in Knox County, Kentucky in the spring of 1934.

The Unquiet Grave

Child 78 A

"The wind doth blow today, my love,
And a few small drops of rain.
I never had but one true-love,
In cold grave she was lain.

"I'll do as much for my true-love
As any young man may.
I'll sit and mourn all at her grave
For twelvemonth and a day."

The twelvemonth and a day being up,
The dead began to speak:
"Oh who sits weeping on my grave,
And will not let me sleep?"

" 'Tis I, my love, sits on your grave,
And will not let you sleep.
For I crave one kiss of your clay-cold lips,
And that is all I seek."

"You crave one kiss of my clay-cold lips,
But my breath smells earthy strong.
If you have one kiss from my clay-cold lips
Your time will not be long.

" 'Tis down in yonder garden green,
Love, where we used to walk.
The finest flower that ere was seen,
Is withered to the stalk.

"The stalk is withered dry, my love,
So will our hearts decay.
So make yourself content, my love,
Till God calls you away."

A memorial reconstruction with genders altered and the wish granted.

Child 78 B

"How cold the wind do[th] blow, dear love,
And see the drops of rain!
I never had but one true-love,
In the green wood he was slain.

"I would do as much for my own true-love
As in my power doth lay;
I would sit and mourn all on his grave
For twelvemonth and a day."

A twelvemonth and a day being past,
His ghost did rise and speak:
"What makes you mourn all on my grave?
For you will not let me sleep."

"It is not your gold I want, dear love,
Nor yet your wealth I crave;
But one kiss from your lily-white lips
Is all I wish to have.

"Your lips are cold as clay, dear love,
Your breath doth smell so strong;"
"I am afraid, my pretty, pretty maid,
Your time will not be long."

Child 78 D

"Proud Boreas makes a hideous noise,
Loud roars the fatal fleed.   *fleed = flood*
I loved never a love but one,
In the church-yard she lies dead.

"But I will do for my love's sake
What other young men may;
I'll sit and mourn upon her grave,
A twelvemonth and a day."

A twelvemonth and a day being past,
The ghost began to speak:
"Why sit ye here upon my grave,
And will not let me sleep?"

"One kiss of your lily-white lips
Is all that I do crave;
And one kiss of your lily-white lips
Is all that I would have."

"Your breath is as the roses sweet,
Mine as the sulpher strong;
If you get one kiss of my lips,
Your days would not be long.

"Mind notye the day, Willie,
Sin you and I did walk?   *Sin = since*
The first and flower that we did pu[ll]
Was withered at the stalk."

"Flowers will fade and die, my dear,
Aye, as the tears will turn;
And since I've lost my own sweet-heart,
I'll never cease but mourn."

"Lament nae mair for me, my love,   *nae mair = no more*
The powers we must obey;
But hoist up one sail to the wind,
Your ship must sail away."

The Wind Blew Up, the Wind Blew Down

American version (1934), *Ballad Book*, p. 175

The wind blew up, the wind blew down
It brought some drops of rain,
My own true love is only one,
And she in the grave has lain,
And she in the grave has lain.

Ah, weep your tear and make a moan,
As many a gay youth may,
And sit and grieve upon her grave,
For a season and a day.
(*Repeat the last line of each stanza.*)

And when the season's past and gone,
The fair young maid did say,
"What man is weeping on my grave,
The night and most the day?"

" 'Tis I, 'tis I, my fair young love,
Who can no longer sleep,
For want of a kiss of your darling lips,
The day and the night I seek."

"Cold clay am I, my lips cold clay,
To kiss them would be wrong,
For if you go against God's law,
Your time will not be long.

"See there, see there, the sun has set,
The day has passed fore'er,
You cannot bring it back again,
By foul means or by fair.

"See there, alas, the garden green,
Where often we did walk,
The fairest flower that e'er was seen
Is withered to the stalk.

"Our own hearts, too, will die, my love,
And like the stalk decay,
So all that you can do, my love,
Is to wait your dyin' day."

45

The Three Ravens

Child no. 26. *Brown Collection* no. 9. Coffin no. 26. Randolph no. 9.

A ballad which did not circulate as widely as many others, but which is widely accepted as having come down from its medieval origin relatively uncontaminated. The number of ravens present changed in the course of its transmission, from two to three and probably (depending upon circumstance) back again. It is one of the very best, if also one of the most unsettling, in the group of traditional English ballads to have come down to us. Its American reputation rests on the somewhat truncated and disappointing version printed below, which has enjoyed a measure of popularity probably at least in part because its more graphic medieval ancestors are not well known.

Twa Corbies

Child 26 A

As I was walking all alane,   *alane = alone*
I heard twa corbies making a mane,   *twa = two; corbies = ravens*
The tane unto t'other say,   *tane = one*
"Where sall we gang and dine to-day?"   *sall = shall; gang = go*

"In behint yon auld fail dyke,   *behint = behind*
I wot there lies a new slain knight.   *wot = know*
And naebody kens that he lies there,   *kens = knows*
But his hawk, his hound, and lady fair.

"His hound is to the hunting gane,   *gane = gone*
His hawk to fetch the wild-fowl hame,   *hame = home*
His lady's te'en another mate,
Se we may make our dinner sweet.

"Ye'll sit on his white hause-bane,   *hause-bane = neck bone*
And I'll pick out his bonny blue een.
Wi ae lock o his gowden hair   trans. = *with one lock of his golden hair*
We'll theek our nest when it grows bare.   *theek = thatch*

Many a one for him makes mane,
But nane sall ken where he is gane.   trans. = *but none shall know where he is gone*
Oer his white banes, when they are bare,
The wind sall blaw for evermair."   *sall blaw* = *shall blow*

The Three Ravens

Child 26 B

There were three rauens sat on a tree,
Downe a downe, hey down, hey downe
There were three reuens sat on a tree
Downe a downe, hay down, hay downe
There were three ravens sat on a tree,
With a downe
There were three rauens sat on a tree
They were as blacke as they might be.
With a downe derrie, derrie, derrie, downe, downe.

The one of them said to his mate,
"Where shall we our breakfast take?"

"Down in yonder greene field
There lies a knight slain vndir his shield.

His hounds they lie downe at his feete,
So well they can their master keepe.

His haukes they fly so eagerly,
There's no fowle dare him come nie."   *nie* = *near*

Downe there comes a fallow doe,
As great with young as she might goe.

She lift vp his bloudy hed,
And kist his wounds that were so red.

She got him vp vpon her backe,
And carried him to earthen lake.

She buried him before the prime,
She was dead herself ere euen-song time.

God send every gentleman,
Such haukes, such hounds, and such a leman.   *leman = lover*

Willie McGee McGaw

American version (date uncertain), *Ballad Book*, p. 103

Three old crows sat on a tree,
Caw, caw, caw,
Three old crows sat on a tree,
Willie McGee McGaw.
Three old crows sat on a tree,
They was black as black could be,
Willie McGee McGee McGaw,
Willie McGee McGaw.

"I know where we find some food,"
Caw, caw, caw,
"I know where we find some food,"
Willie McGee McGaw.
"I know where we find some food,
Yonder in the cool green wood."
Willie McGee McGee McGaw,
Willie McGee McGaw.

"Come and taste it, you can tell
It is cooked very well."

Mr. Crow to Miz Crow said:
"I will eat it, alive or dead."

Horse and rider side by side,
It was morning when they died.

X

Carols

Carols enjoy an association with Christmas and also with childhood which has preserved their modern popularity, but in spite of my first choice here, it is important to remember that in the medieval period carols were by no means confined to Christmas, or associated with childhood. Though the number of Christmas carols increased late in the period, carols generally were associated more often with feast days, and with public entertainment and dance. As Green points out, as a general rule they seem not to have been performed professionally by minstrels, but were usually sung with conviviality, and by any and all. The great majority of the 500 or so carols (the word originally meant "a dance") which have come down to us are both religious and fifteenth-century, and it is quite probable that the genre began, as Richard L. Greene argued, as songs performed in association with dance, in which, in later times, a leader sang the verses and was answered by the dancers who sang the burden or refrain. This burden, which was the distinguishing mark of the carol, was sung at the beginning, and then again after each stanza, during which the dancers often seem to have been in motion, dancing in a circle while the burden was sung, and in some cases at least, standing motionless (or marking time) while the leader sang the stanzas (though there were no rules, variation was everywhere, and the order could easily have been reversed). Over its history, the verse forms of both burden and stanzas differed widely, though the burden often rhymes with the last line of the stanzas. An alternative but far less compelling view by Rossell Hope Robbins suggests that carols originated in Latin processional hymns. Attempts to find a middle ground between these theories have not been notably successful, though during the medieval period dances were performed in churches as part of the liturgy on certain occasions, and these may have been informed by the secular conventions Greene noted. But carols came to stand on their own, and their association with dance (or procession) was not observed universally.

But perhaps more than any other genre, we have yet fully to understand the importance and the several uses of these very social song-poems, known as carols, in late medieval British culture. Greene's great edition, the notes to which give repeated evidence of their broad cultural popularity, located almost 500, and, as with ballads, others and other versions must certainly have perished, though unlike ballads they were frequently written down, often in manuscripts associated with religious houses, at least in part because of the communal and social ways in which they were performed. Since carols almost by definition involved communal performance (unlike most lyrics), their presence must have been widely felt, but some contexts were evidently more private, and certain carols could serve as lullabies or even as love songs: the presence of a refrain did not finally enforce communal performance, after all, though it often suggests it. Their frequent association with dance, however, has placed them outside the orbit of many studies of late medieval music or poetry, and so marginalized, at least in academic circles, what must have been an important, and possibly even a central, art form.

In any event, as carols detached from the dance they maintained an association with the ballad, whose meter and stanza structure they sometimes imitated, further evidence, if any was needed, that large numbers of now-lost ballads circulated in the period. Partly because of their origin and development, carols often present religious attitudes and topoi, and even liturgical uses, and as entertainments they often figured at religious feasts, such as Assumption or Christmas, though they are also associated with Advent, Epiphany, Candlemas, Christ's mother and father and his Passion, the saints, the Trinity, the Eucharist, the mass, Corpus Christi, Purgatory, Domesday, Repentance, satire, women, politics and marriage, among other topics. Their scope was as broad as their authors' wit, and their cultivated religious associations did not prevent a powerful secular impact, if usually, as the manuscripts attest, in connection with shared and social entertainment.

The central text remains Richard L. Greene, ed., *The Early English Carols*, second edition (Oxford: Clarendon Press, 1977). I am indebted both to Greene's edition, and to his entry for "Carols" in Albert E. Hartung, ed., *A Manual of the Writings in Middle English, 1050–1500* (New Haven: Connecticut Academy of Arts and Sciences, 1980), VI, pp. 1743–52 and 1923–2018. For Rossell Hope Robbins' alternative explanation of the carols' origin see his "Middle English Carols as Processional Hymns," *Studies in Philology* 56 (1959): 559–82, and Douglas Gray, "Fifteenth-Century Lyrics and Carols," in Helen Cooney, ed., *Nation, Court and Culture: New Essays on Fifteenth-Century Poetry* (Dublin: Four Courts Press, 2001), pp. 168–83.

46

IMEV 1004. Bodleian Library, Oxford. MS Arch. Selden B. 26 (*SC* 3340), fol. 8. Davies no. 116. Greene no. 5.

Another energetic Christmas carol (see no. 11 above) in which religious sentiment mixes easily with a somewhat more secular tone. Notice also the reference to Christ's redemptive purpose, and so indirectly, even in this most joyous of lyrics, to his Passion and death. (See figure 6, p. 160.)

Go day, go day,   Go day = Good day
My lord Syre Cristemasse, go day!

Go day, Syre Cristemas, our kyng,
For euery man, both olde and yynge,
Ys glad and blithe of your comynge.

Go day . . .

Godys Sone, so moche of myght,
Fram heuen to erthe dovn is lyght   dovn = down,
And borne ys of a mayde so bryght.   bryght = radiant, beautiful

Go day . . .

Heuen and erthe and also helle,   helle = purgatory
And alle that euer in hem dwelle,
Of your comynge they beth ful snelle.   snelle = active (with joy)

Go day . . .

Of your comynge this clerkys fynde:
Ye come to saue al mankynde,
And of here balys hem vnbynde.   balys = sufferings

Go day . . .

Alle maner of merthes we wole make
And solas to oure hertys take,
My semely Lorde, for youre sake.

Go day . . .

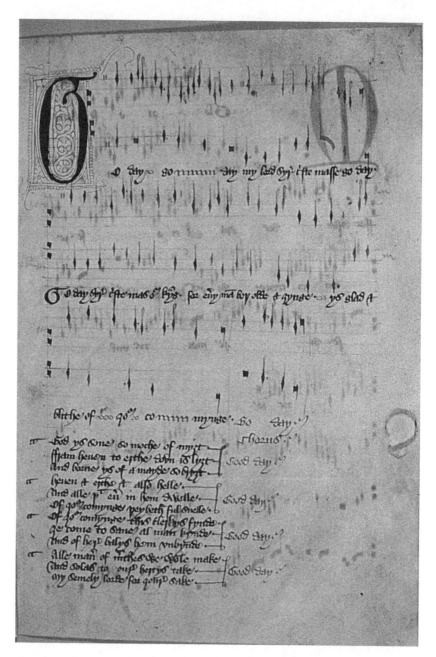

Figure 6 Bodleian Library MS Arch. Selden B 26 (*SC* 3340), folio 8. A most important fifteenth-century English manuscript containing secular music which includes, among other items, the Christmas carol "Good Day!" (no. 46), reproduced here, and the popular patriotic "Agincourt Carol" (no. 49), which celebrated King Henry V's 1415 victory.

47

IMEV 1363. Balliol College, Oxford. MS 354, fol. 230v. Greene no. 241.

A spirited and joyous medieval Annunciation carol, preserved in an early sixteenth-century manuscript which also contains nos 11 and 24, above. It is very much a lyric in praise of the Blessed Virgin, but one in whose central and climactic point is Mary's free acceptance of God's offer (transmitted through the angel) to become Christ's mother. The song joyously realizes the popular and widely-accepted theological teaching that Mary freely accepted the role offered to her, and also preserved her virginity before, during, and after Christ's birth. The repeated invitation to the audience to know, understand, and share in the joyful celebration of the feast day is predicated on the further teaching that in so doing Mary acted as a representative for all of women, indeed for all of humankind, so that all persons share in her honor.

What, hard ye not? The Kyng of Jhrewsalem
Is now born in Bethelem.

I shall you tell a gret mervayll,
How an angell, for owr avayll,
Com to a mayd and said: "All hayll!"

What, hard ye not . . .

"All hayll!" he said, and "full of grace,
God is with the now in this place,
A child thou shalt bere in lytill space."   *lytill space = very soon*

What, hard ye not . . .

"A child?" she said, "How may that be?
Ther had never no man knowlage of me."
"The Holy Gost," he said, "shall light in the."

What, hard ye not . . .

"And as thou art, so shall thow be,"
The angell sayd, "in virgynite,
Before and after in euery degree."

What, hard ye not . . .

The mayd answered the angell agayn:
"Yf God will that this be sayn,   *sayn* = *said*
The wordes be to me ffull fayn."   *fayn* = *glad*

What, hard ye not . . .

Now will we alle, in reioysynge,
That we haue hard this good tydyng,
To that child *"Te Deum"* synge.   Te Deum = *a Latin hymn of praise to God*

48

IMEV 2654. British Library, London. MS Sloane 1584, fol. 45v. Greene no. 446.

An intentionally quite hilarious fifteenth-century amorous carol, which easily mixes erotic physical description and psychological attitudes. Spoken in a woman's voice, but was it actually written by a woman?

Troly Lole

So well ys me begone,　　　　　　　　trans. = *so fortunate am I*
Troly lole,
So well ys me begone,　　　　　　　　begone = *provided for*
Troly loly.

Off seruyng men I wyll begyne,
Troly loley,
For they goo mynyon trym,　　　　　*mynyon trim = daintily trim* (Greene)
Troly loley.

Off mett and drynk and feyr clothyng,
Troly loley,
By dere God, I want none,
Troly loley.

His bonet is of fyne scarlett,
Troly loley.
With here as black as geitt,　　　　　here = *hair;* geitt = *jet*
Troly lolye.

His dublett ys of fyne satyne,　　　　*dublett = doublet, a tight-fitting jacket*
Troly lolye,
Hys shertt well mayd and tryme,
Troly lolye.

His coytt itt is so tryme and rownde,　*coytt = coat;* rownde = *rownd, full*
Troly lolye,
His kysse is worth a hundred pounde,
Troly loly.

His hoysse are of Londoun black,   *hoysse* = *stockings; are* = MS omission
Troly lolye,
In hyme ther ys no lack,
Troly lolye.

His face yt ys so lyk a man,
Troly lolye,
Who can butt love hyme than?
Troly lolye.

Whersoeuer he bee, he hath my hert,
Troly loly,
And shall to deth depart,
Troly lolye.

So well ys me begone,
Troly loly,
So well ys me begone,
Troly loly.

49

IMEV 2716. Bodleian Library, Oxford. MS Arch. Selden B. 26 (*SC* 3340), fol. 17v–18. Davies no. 80. Duncan B no. 132. Greene no. 426.

The battle of Agincourt, a three-and-a-half-hour engagement, was fought on October 25, 1415. The traditionally round, and probably untrustworthy, medieval figures are these: England suffered 100 killed or wounded, 13 of whom were men-at-arms; France suffered 7,000 killed, and 1,000 prisoners. A mixture of soft ground after heavy rains, Welsh archers with their backs to the wall and as deadly with the mace as with the bow, and more than either of these, the utter incompetence of a packed French charge which, in a narrow field of battle, left no room for maneuver or even for effective fighting, all contributed to the extraordinary and overwhelming English victory which King Henry V, much to the irritation of the French, repeatedly attributed to God's help alone.

Greene suggests that the repeated thanks to God in this carol suggest clerical authorship, and would not have violated Henry's insistence that his victory was due to God alone. If so, it was a victory marred, to the modern eye, by Henry's massacre of all but the noblest (and so most valuable) of his prisoners when he found himself under renewed attack, but unsurprisingly, praise in England was more or less universal, and included this carol. But the carol does attest to the growth of national sentiment and to the sense of an English nation, in a way found in relatively few earlier medieval poems, but which was to survive even the so-called War of the Roses (1455–87), which pitted the House of Lancaster against that of York, and whose conclusion, when King Henry VII (1457–1509, reigned 1485–1509) assumed the throne, effectively moved the medieval period toward a close, at least in England.

See Wolfgang G. Müller, "The Battle of Agincourt in Carol and Ballad," *Fifteenth-Century Studies* 8 (1983): 159–78. In the text which follows I have moved the third stanza up from its manuscript position at the end of the poem.

The Agincourt Carol

Deo gracias Anglia   trans. = England, give thanks to God for victory
Redde pro victoria.

Owre kynge went forth to Normandy,
With grace and myght of chyualry.
Ther God for hym wrought mervelusy,
Wherfore Englonde may calle and cry,

Deo gracias . . .

He sette a sege, the sothe for to say,   *sege = seige*
To Harflu, tovne with ryal aray.   *tovne = town*
That tovne he wan and made a fray,
That Fraunce shal rywe tyl domesday.

Deo gracias . . .

Than went oure kynge, with alle his oste,   *oste = host*
Thorwe Fraunce, for alle the Frenshe boste.
He spared no drede of lest ne moste,
Tyl he come to Agincourt coste.   *coste = area around*

Deo gracias . . .

Than, forsoth, that knyght comely,   *forsoth = truly, in truth; comely = attractive*
In Agincourt feld he faught manly,
Thorw grace of God most myghty,
He had bothe the felde and the victory.

Deo gracias . . .

There dukys and erlys, lorde and barone,
Were take and slayne, and that wel sone,   *wel sone = very quickly*
And summe were ladde into Lundone,
With joye and merthe and grete renone.   *renone = acclaim, renown*

Deo gracias . . .

Now gracious God, he saue oure kynge,   *he saue = may he save*
His peple, and alle his wel-wyllynge,   *wel-wyllynge = well wishers*
Yef hym gode lyfe and gode endynge,   *Yef = give; gode endynge = a good death*
That we with merth mowe sauely synge,   *sauely = with safety*

Deo gracias . . .

50

Supplement 409.5. British Library, London. Additional MS 31922, fol. 37v.
Davies no. 180. Greene no. 448.

A renaissance carol, attributed in the sixteenth-century manuscript to King
Henry VIII (1491–1547, reigned 1509–47), which remains clearly indebted to
the medieval carol. The imagery carries still semi-religious connotations, here
fading to secular, with the holly and the ivy representing man and woman
respectively. Greene points out that the first line of the burden was a folk-
saying indicating "for ever," appropriate in a carol which protested faithfulness.
The assurance at the end of the poem proved, in Henry's case, to be entirely
conventional.

The Holly and the Ivy

Grene growith the holy,   holy = holly
So doth the iue,   iue = ivy
Thow wynter blastys blow neuer so hye,
Grene growth the holy.

As the holly grouth grene,
And neuer chaungyth hew,
So I am, euer hath bene,
Vnto my lady trew.

Grene growith . . .

As the holy grouth grene
With iue all alone,
When flowerys cannot be sene,
And grenewode leuys be gone.

Grene growith . . .

Now vnto my lady
Promyse to her I make,
Frome all other only
To her I me betake.

Grene growith . . .

Adew, myne owne lady,
Adew, my specyall,
Who hath my hart trewly,
Be suere, and euer shall.   *suere = sure*

Appendix A: Some Lyrics of Geoffrey Chaucer

The most accomplished poet of his, and many later, generations, Geoffrey Chaucer (d. 1400) is now best known for his brilliant collection of narratives called the *Canterbury Tales*, just as he was in earlier centuries for his long narrative love poem *Troilus and Criseyde*. I have included in this appendix a few examples of what Chaucer called "ballades," the name derived from the French, where, however, the word usually designated a poem with three seven- or eight-line stanzas, each employing the same rhymes, and each ending with the same line, which thus functioned as a refrain. In Middle English rules were not so strict, and as the editors of the Variorum Edition of these lyrics point out, "almost any stanzaic poem could be called a ballade." But Chaucer wrote many of his short poems (and certain of his longer narratives) in what became known as rhyme royal, seven-line stanzas, rhyming ababbcc, with five (or four) of the ten syllables stressed.

Chaucer rarely wrote in a genre he did not adapt and improve, and that is true of his lyrics, too. Occasionally, in his narrative texts, and particularly at an important or crucial moment, he signals powerful emotion by inscribing an "embedded lyric," a short lyrical outburst which serves to focus and reveal an inner attitude, and lend power and significance to the scene in which it appears. I have selected two of these and printed them below. Scholars are inclined to think that Chaucer wrote only one religious lyric, "An ABC" inscribed to Mary, and adapted from a long allegorical poem by Guillaume de Deguilleville, but the "Invocatio ad Mariam" in the Prologue to the *Second Nun's Tale* in the *Canterbury Tales* forms a second, the last three stanzas in the Prioress' Prologue a third. I have printed another here.

Except where noted (that is, in the case of the embedded lyrics), I have edited Chaucer's poems from volume V of the Variorum Edition, George B. Pace and Alfred David, eds., *The Minor Poems: Part One* (Norman, Okla.: University of Oklahoma Press, 1982). I am indebted to Pace and David's introductions throughout, including their treatment of the ballade, pp. 5–6. I am further indebted to V. J. Scattergood's chapter "The Short Poems," in *The Shorter Poems*, ed. A. J. Minnis, et al., Oxford Guides to Chaucer (Oxford: Clarendon Press, 1995), pp. 455–512. On Chaucer's embedded lyrics see Arthur K. Moore, "Chaucer's Lost Songs," *Journal of English and Germanic Philology* 48 (1949): 196–208, and "Chaucer's Use of Lyric as an Ornament of Style," *Comparative Literature* 3 (1951): 32–46. There are two related and useful studies by Julia Boffey, "The Reputation and Circulation of Chaucer's Lyrics in the Fifteenth Century," *Chaucer Review* 28 (1993): 23–40, reprinted in Daniel J. Pinti, ed., *Writing after Chaucer: Essential Readings in Chaucer and the Fifteenth Century*, Basic Reading in Chaucer and His Time (New York and London: Garland, 1998), pp. 127–44; and "The Lyrics in Chaucer's Longer Poems," *Poetica* 37 (1993): 15–37.

A1

Truth

"Truth" is one of those poems which collects stories around it, and as a result becomes famous, at least for a time. According to Shirley, an early scribe who copied many of Chaucer's works, Chaucer wrote the poem "upon his deathbed, and in great anguish." But the story seems unlikely. For one thing, the poem may well have existed both with and without the Envoy – and the version that Shirley knew was probably without, since it is unlikely that, *in extremis*, even Chaucer would have adopted the light, almost bantering tone of the Envoy to his younger friend, Sir Philip de la Vache, whose spirits he appears to be raising after having been, perhaps like Chaucer himself, disappointed at court. He plays on his friend's name (Vache means "cow"), when he commands him to come out of his stall, but Shirley responded rather to the poem's lofty tone, a tone which seems to echo the *De consolatione* of the early sixth-century philosopher Boethius, whom Chaucer knew and translated, and who certainly informed certain of his fictions, like the *Knight's Tale*. The poem itself, written in rhyme royal, is concerned with the value of personal integrity in the face of instability and falseness. This Chaucerian lyric entered the canon of English literature relatively early, and there is reason to believe that it was known (in a slightly corrupt version) by Shakespeare, Jonson, and Milton, among others.

The idea that Chaucer revised this lyric is not universally accepted. See Ralph Hanna III, "Authorial Versions, Rolling Revision and Scribal Error? Or, the Truth About *Truth*," *Studies in the Age of Chaucer* 10 (1988): 23–40. But the matter is far from closed.

Fle fro the pres and dwelle with sothfastnesse.	*pres = crowd*
Suffise thin owen thing though it be smal.	*thing = possessions*
For horde hathe hate, and clymbyng tykelnesse,	*horde = hoarding;* *tykelnesse = instability*
Prees hathe envye, and wele blent oueral.	*wele = prosperity; blent = blinds*
Sauoure no more thanne the byhoue schal	*the byhoue = behoves thee*
Reule weel thiself, that other folk canst rede,	*rede = advise*
And trouthe the schal delyuere, it is no drede.	*the = MS omission;* *delyuere = free*

Tempest the nought al croked to redress,	*Tempest = trouble; croked = wrongs*
In trust of hire that tourneth as a bal,	*hire = fortune*

Myche wele stant in litel besynesse.

Bewar therfore to spurne ageyns an al.   *spurne . . . al = kick a nail*

Stryue not as dothe the crokke with the wal,   *crokke = crock (proverbial)*

Daunte thi self that dauntest otheres dede,   *Daunte = rule; dede = deeds*

And trouthe the shal delyuere, it is no drede.   *the = MS omission*

That the is sente receyue in buxhumnesse,   *buxhumnesse = obedience*

The wrestlyng for the world axeth a fal,

Here is non home, here nys but wyldernesse,   *nys = is not*

Forthe, Pylgryme, forthe! Forthe beste out of thi stal!

Knowe thi contre, lok vp, thonk God of al,

Holde the heyeweye, and lat thi gost the   *heyeweye = highway;*

   lede,   *gost = spirit, soul*

And trouthe the shal delyuere, it is no drede.   *the = MS omission*

Envoy

Therfore, thou Vache, leue thine olde   *Vache = Sir Philip de la Vache*

   wrechedenesse

Vnto the world, leue now to be thral.

Crie Hym mercy, that of His hie godnesse   *hie = high*

Made the of nought, and in especial

Drawe vnto Hym and pray in general

For the and eke for other, heuenlyche   *eke = also; other = others;*

   mede,   *mede = reward*

And trouthe the shal delyuere, it is no drede.   *the = MS omission*

A2

The Complaint of Chaucer to his Purse

Chaucerians agree that this rhyme royal poem was indeed written with a purpose – talk about poetic intention! – and that was when the 1399 removal of King Richard II, and the installation of King Henry IV, interrupted the crown payments to which Chaucer had become entitled. What is unclear is how effective it proved to be. Chaucer probably died in October, 1400, and though his royal grant from Henry is dated October, 1399, it appears to have been antedated, and February 1400 seems more probable. Subsequently, Chaucer did receive two crown payments before he died, but, as his life records reveal, neither was in the amount due him.

Still, the poem itself is a treat – not only does it play upon the secular tradition of the lover's complaint to his disdainful lady, but its imagery ("Quene of comfort") engages directly that of the religious lyric, on which the secular love-tradition ("voucheth sauf this day") also drew. It is difficult to know how far to pursue topical allusion in this poem (does "Oute of this tovne" really refer to the poet escaping Westminster?), but the poem is one of the most effective and amusing of his "begging poems" to come down to us.

See Sumner J. Ferris, "The Date of Chaucer's Final Annuity and 'The Complaint to his Empty Purse,'" *Modern Philology* 65 (1967): 45–52; Andrew J. Finnel, "The Poet as Sunday Man: 'The Complaint of Chaucer to his Purse,'" *Chaucer Review*, 8 (1973): 147–58; and Paul Strohm, "Saving the Appearances: Chaucer's 'Purse' and the Fabrication of the Lancastrian Claim," in *Hochon's Arrow* (Princeton: Princeton University Press, 1992), pp. 75–94.

See further Martin M. Crow and Clair C. Olson, eds., *Chaucer Life Records* (Austin: University of Texas Press, and Oxford: Oxford University Press, 1966); the best life of Chaucer is by Derek Pearsall, *The Life of Geoffrey Chaucer*, Blackwell Critical Biographies 1 (Oxford and Cambridge, Mass.: Blackwell, 1992).

To yow, my purse, and to noon other wight	*wight = creature, person*
Complayn I, for ye be my lady dere,	
I am so sory now that ye been lyght,	*lyght = light, loose (in manner)*
For certes, but yf ye make me hevy chere,	*but yf = unless; hevy chere = sober up*
Me were as leef be layde vpon my bere,	*as leef = rather*
For whiche vnto your mercy thus I crye,	
Beeth hevy ayeyne, or elles mote I dye!	*ayeyne = again*

Now voucheth sauf this day, or hit be nyght,   *voucheth sauf = grant, promise*
That, I of yow, the blisful soune may here   *soune = sound*
Or see your colour, lyke the sonne bryght,
That of yelownesse hadde neuer pere.   *pere = equal*
Ye be my lyfe, ye be myn hertys stere,
Quene of comfort and of good companye,
Beth heuy ayeyne, or elles moote I dye!

Now purse, that ben to me my lyves lyght,
And saueour as doun in this worlde here,
Oute of this tovne helpe me thurgh your myght
Syn that ye wole nat bene my tresorere.
For I am shave as nye as is a   *shave . . . frere = as shaved (of money)*
    frere,   *as a friar's head is of hair*
But yet I pray vnto your curtesye,
Beth hevy ayen, or elles moote I dye!

LENVOY DE CHAUCER
   O conquerour of Brutes Albyon!   *Brutes Albyon = Britain*
Whiche that by lygne and free eleccion   *lygne = lineage*
Been verray kynge, this song to yow I sende   *verray = true*
And ye that mowen alle oure harmes amende,   *mowen = may*
Haue mynde vpon my supplicacion.

A3

To Rosemounde

There is still a shade of doubt concerning Chaucer's authorship of this lively and engaging poem which, untypically for Chaucer but common enough for Middle English lyrics generally, is preserved in only one manuscript. The real question is whether it is sexist or charming, and the answer really depends on whom it was written for. Is "Rosemounde" a conventional name chosen to give no offence (a trick it perhaps no longer accomplishes), or was the poem inscribed for Queen Isabella, King Richard II's seven-year-old child bride, who came to London in 1396 (in which case it can be read as sophisticated and amusing)? "Mapamonde," which means simply map of the world (round only because it was drawn within a circle), may be innocent of any physical connotation, and the reference to a "pike . . . in galauntyne" (a cold, jellied sauce) need not exclude the suggestion that the poem was written for a child, even if there is a topical allusion in it – after all, what seven-year-old does not know what she likes to eat? But the poem may not refer to anyone, and is probably nothing more or less than a sophisticated and very amusing parody of a lover's complaint.

For a defense of the Queen Isabella thesis see Rossell Hope Robbins, "Chaucer's 'To Rosemounde'," *Studies in the Literary Imagination*, 4 (1971): 73–81.

Ma dame, ye ben of al beaute shryne	
As fer cercled is the mapamonde.	*mapamonde = map of the world*
For as the cristall glorious ye shyne,	
And like ruby ben your chekys rounde.	
Therwyth ye ben so mery and so iocunde	*iocunde = jolly*
That at a reuell whan that I se you dance	*reuell = revel*
It is an oynement vnto my wounde,	
Thogh ye to me ne do no daliance.	*do . . . daliance = give no encouragement*

For thogh I wepe of teres ful a tyne,	*tyne = barrel*
Yet may that wo myn herte nat confounde.	*wo = woe, pain*
Your semy voys, that ye so small out	*semy = fine, delicate;*
twyne,	*out twyne = force (twist) out*
Makyth my thoght in ioy and blys habounde.	*habounde = abound*
So curtaysly I go wyth loue bounde	
That to myself I sey in my penaunce:	

"Suffyseth me to loue you Rosemounde,
Thogh ye to me ne do no daliaunce."

Nas neuer pyk walwed in
   galauntyne

*pyk = pike; walwed = smothered
(in a sauce)*

As I in loue am walwed and i-wounde.

For whych ful ofte I of myself deuyne

deuyne = suppose, understand

That I am trew Tristam the
   secunde.

*Tristram = the stereotype of the
suffering lover*

My loue may not refreyde nor
   affounde,

*refreyde . . . affounde = turn
cold or numb*

I brenne ay in an amorouse plesaunce.

ay = ever

Do what you lyst, I wyl your thral be founde,

thral = slave

Thogh ye to me ne do no daliaunce.

A4

Lak of Stedfastnesse

Written in rhyme royal, and sometimes said to be Chaucer's only manifestly political poem, "Lak of Stedfastnesse" was almost certainly directed to King Richard II during one of the many crises which first infected, and then finally overcame, his very troubled reign, but it is impossible to say which one. Its moral tone and Boethian exhortation suggest a date very late indeed in Richard's monarchy, but its preservation in 15 fifteenth-century manuscripts suggests that it enjoyed a measure of popularity unconnected to the political circumstances which called it forth.

See Liam O. Purdon, "Chaucer's *Lak of Stedfastnesse*: A Revalorization of the Word," in Julian N. Wasserman and Lois Roney, eds., *Sign, Sentence, Discourse: Language in Medieval Thought and Literature* (Syracuse, N.Y.: Syracuse University Press, 1989), pp. 144–52, for a reading which treats the important role of language in the poem, and for the poem's political context, see V. J. Scattergood, "Social and Political Issues in Chaucer: An Approach to *Lak of Stedfastnesse*," *Chaucer Review* 21 (1987): 469–75; George B. Pace, "Chaucer's *Lak of Stedfastnesse*," *Studies in Bibliography* 4 (1951–2): 105–22; and Paul Srohm, "The Textual Environment of Chaucer's 'Lak of Stedfastnesse,'" in *Hochon's Arrow* (Princeton: Princeton University Press, 1992), pp. 57–74.

Sumtyme the world was so steadfast and stable
That mannes worde was obligacion,   *obligacion = his bond*
And nowe it is so false and deseiuable   *deseiuable = deceiving*
That worde and dede, as in conclusion,
Is nothing lyke – for turned vp-so-doun
Is all this worlde for mede and wilfulnesse –   *mede = bribery*
That al is lost for lak of stedfastnesse.

What maketh this world to be so veriable   *veriable = changing*
But lust that folke haue in discencion?   *lust = pleasure; discencion = dissenting*
For amonge vs now a man is holde vnable
But yif he can by som collusion   *But yif = unless*
Do his neyghburgh wrong or oppression.   *neyghburgh = neighbor*
What causeth this but wilfull wrechidnesse
That al is lost for lak of stedfastnesse?

Trouthe is putte doun, resoun is holden fable,
Vertu hath now no domynacion,
Pite exiled, no man is merciable,
Through couetise is blent discrescioun.
The worlde hath made a permutacion,   *permutacion = change*
Fro right to wrong, fro trought to fikelnesse,   *trought = integrity*
That al is lost for lak of stedfastnesse.

ENVOY TO KING RICHARD
O Prince, desire to be honurable!
Cherice thi folk and hate extorcioun!   *Cherice = cherish*
Suffre nothing that may be repreuable   *repreuable = reprehensible*
To thine estaat doen in thi regioun!   *doen = done*
Shewe forth thy swerde of Castigacioun!   *swerde = sword*
Drede God. Do Law. Love truthe and worthynesse,   *Do = enforce*
And wed thi folk ayen to stedfastnesse!

Explicit.

A5

Embedded Lyric A

Geoffrey Chaucer, d. 1400, *Man of Law's Tale*, II (B1) 841–54, from the *Canterbury Tales*.

This is an embedded lyric found in a narrative text (in this case Chaucer's *Man of Law's Tale*) which, though not set out as a lyric, both draws upon and re-creates the power, devout impulse, and brevity which are present too in certain Marian lyrics. The lines appear at a crucial moment in the tale, altogether one of Chaucer's most religious narratives, when Chaucer has stopped the action so as to insert into his text what amounts to a short, powerful lyric in praise of the Blessed Virgin. This is one of those instances in Middle English literature when we see Chaucer employ a religious lyric for narrative and dramatic effect, and here it functions both as a prayer for help, and also as a poem in praise of Mary.

I have edited this text from the Hengwrt manuscript (following Paul G. Ruggiers' University of Oklahoma Press edition, 1979), and have printed my read-ing of "woman" in line 7, instead of the usual reading of "wo man" (i.e., "woe [which] man"), a choice which seems to me indicated by context and tone of the narrative. I have defended this reading in "Chaucer's *Man of Law's Tale* 847: A Conjectural Emendation," *Chaucer Review* 20 (1985): 68–9, objected to by Alasdair A. MacDonald, "Chaucer's *Man of Law's Tale* 847: A Reconsideration," *Chaucer Review* 22 (1988): 246–9, and my response, "Chaucer's *Man of Law's Tale* 847: A Rejoinder," *Chaucer Review* 22 (1988): 332–4.

"Moder," quod she, "and mayden bright, Marie,
Sooth is that thurgh wommans eggement, *eggement = temptation*
Mankynde was lorn, and dampned ay to dye, *lorn = lost; ay = ever*
For which thy child was on a croys yrent. *yrent = torn*
Thy blisful eyen sawe al his torment –
Thanne is ther no comparisoun bitwene
Thy wo, and any woman may sustene.

"Thow sawe thy child yslayn bifor thyne eyen,
And yet now lyueth my litel child, parfay! *parfay = by faith*
Now, lady bright, to whom alle woful cryen,

Thou glorie of wommanhede, thow faire
    may,
Thow hauen of refut, brighte sterre of day,
Rewe on my child, that of thy gentillesse,
Rewest on euery rewful in distresse."

may = maiden, also the
month May
refut = refuge
Rewe = have pity

A6

Embedded Lyric B

Geoffrey Chaucer, the *Merchant's Tale*, IV (E) 2138–48, from the *Canterbury Tales*.

An embedded lyric from Chaucer's *Merchant's Tale*, again drawn from Paul Ruggiers' edition of the Hengwrt manuscript, in which an old and blind knight, January, marries a young and adventurous woman, May, with the expected result. As he leads her into an enclosed garden January delivers these lines, rooted in the *Canticum canticorum*, which, considered apart from their context, are as felt a declaration of love as anything Chaucer ever wrote. In context, however, the passage manages at once to invite and to disparage love both. The complex connection of the lines to the *Canticum canticorum*, the *Song of Songs*, now often noted, was first developed by Douglas Wurtele, "Ironical Resonances in the *Merchant's Tale*," *Chaucer Review* 13 (1978): 66–79.

"Rys vp, my wyf, my loue, my lady free.
The turtles voys is herd, my dowue swete.
The wynter is goon, with reynes wete.
Com forth now, with thyne eyen Columbyn,
How fairer been thy brestes than is wyn.
The gardyn is enclosed al aboute,
Com forth my white spouse, out of doute,
Thow hast me wounded in myn herte, O Wyf!
No spot of thee ne knew I al my lyf.
Com forth, and lat vs taken oure desport,
I chees thee for my wyf and my confort."

A7

To Adam, My Scribe

Unnamed, and often called "Adam Scryveyne," this epigram (it is hardly a poem, at least as Chaucer usually understands the word) may simply draw upon a medieval tradition of being rude to one's scribe ("Adam" has never been satisfactorily identified in spite of a spate of letters to the *Times Literary Supplement* in 1929), though equally the reference to "thy long lokkes" (though quite possibly conventional) may imply a known individual, who, like the first biblical Adam, has contaminated his master's great work. Chaucer refers to his translation of the late ancient philosopher Boethius ("Boece") and to his great poem *Troilus and Criseyde* ("Troylus").

Adam, scryveyne, if ever it thee befalle,	scryveyne = scribe
Boece or Troylus for to wryten newe,	
Vnder thy long lokkes thowe most haue	lokkes = locks; scalle = a disease
the scalle	of the scalp
But after my makyng thowe wryt more trewe!	But = unless
So oft a-daye I mot thy werk renewe	
It to corect and eke to rubbe and	eke = also; scrape = erase by
scrape,	scraping the parchment
And all is thorugh thy necglygence and rape!	rape = haste (but with a pun)

Appendix B: Poems by William Herebert, Richard Rolle, and John Audelay

Although the majority of Middle English lyrics are anonymous, a number are not, and what follows are representative selections from three very different religious poets, each employing vernacular verse to speak to thoughtful (but perhaps Latinless) laypersons in the hope of moving them to devotion, whether by praising Christ and his mother, or reminding them of their sins, or citing the putative religiousness of great persons, or even by recording an ecstatic awareness of God's divinity. The voices here differ greatly, ranging from homiletic to mystical, from the devout to the affective, and reflect both the poet's religious and theological understanding and his individual caste of mind.

William Herebert

Friar William Herebert, OFM, may have been born sometime after 1270 (when writing about medieval persons the biographer is often reduced to such subjunctives), and was between 1317 and 1319 Lecturer in Theology at the Franciscan House in Oxford where he was the author of 17 Middle English poems (many adapted from hymns) and of a number of polished Latin sermons. He may well have been the friend and sometime colleague of the great medieval thinker, philosopher, and activist, the Franciscan William of Ockham (c.1285–1347), whose social attitudes and theological opinions, but not activist politics, he may have shared. Though the best source for Herebert's later life was written in the sixteenth century, and is so very late, it accords with what little is known, and confirms that he died in or about 1333, and was buried at Hereford, which seems to have been his native convent. Certain of his lyrics seem to have been intended for use in sermons, but others were not, though as a whole his English verse seems to have had a practical bent, sometimes exhibiting a studied, even formal, tone, but as often one powerful and felt.

Some of Herebert's best lyrics are the result of carefully rendering early Latin hymns, whose stately meters are reflected in his own measured verse.

The best recent study of Herebert's life is contained in the edition of his works by Stephen R. Reimer, ed., *The Works of William Herebert, OFM*, Sources and Texts 81 (Toronto: Pontifical Institute of Medieval Studies, 1987), and I am indebted to it for what I have written above. See also Rossell Hope Robbins, "Friar Herebert and the Carol," *Anglia* 75 (1957): 194–8.

B1

Alma Redemptoris Mater

IMEV 1232. British Library MS Additional 46919 *olim* Phillipps MS 8336, fol. 207v. Brown B no. 19. Reimer no. 9.

An early and (for Herebert) a relatively free translation into English of this well-known hymn to Christ's mother, which was sometimes taught to children. The Latin original is referred to in Chaucer's *Prioress' Tale*. I have divided Herebert's long line throughout.

Holy Moder, that bere Cryst,	
Buggere of monkunde,	*Buggere = redeemer*
Thou art gat of heuene blisse,	
That prest wey gyfst and bunde.	*prest = quick; gyfst = give; bunde = at hand*
Thou sterre of se, rer op the uolk	*rer op = raise up; uolk = people*
That rysing haueht in munde.	*haueht = have it; munde = mind*
In the thou bere thyn holy fader,	*fader = father*
That mayden were, after and rather,	*after and rather = before and after*
Wharof so wondreth kunde.	*wondreth kunde = amazed nature*
Of Gabrieles mouthe	*uonge = caught; thylke = that*
Thou uonge thylke "*Aue.*"	
Lesne ous of sunne nouthe,	*trans. = release us now of sin,*
So woe bisecheth the.	*we beseech thee*
AmeN.	

B2

Jesus our Ransom

IMEV 1742. British Library MS Additional 46919 *olim* Phillipps MS 8336, fol. 209v. Brown B no. 24. Reimer no. 14.

An English translation of an early seventh-century Latin hymn on Christ's Ascension, here constructed in short lines so as to lend itself to a meditative, introspective reading. Thus understood, it does not lend itself to what Brown called "pulpit use." I have read U/u (V/v) as F/f.

Iesu our raunsoun,	
Loue and longynge,	
Louerd God Almyhti,	
Whrouhte of alle thinge.	
Flesh thou nome,	*nome* = took
And mon bicome	
In times endinge.	
What milsfolnesse awalde	*milsfolnesse* = MS *milfolnesse* = mercy;
the,	*awalde* = availed
That oure sunnes bere,	*sunnes* = sins
So bitter deth to tholien,	*tholien* = suffer
From sunne ous uor t'arere?	*t'arere* = to lift up
Helle clos thou thorledest	trans. = through hell's gates thou lead
And bouhtest thine of bondes.	*of* = out of
Wyht gret nobleye	*Wyht* = with
Thou opsteye	*opsteye* = ascended
To thy Fader ryht honde.	*Fader* = father's
Thylke mylse nede the	*Thylke mylse* = that mercy
T'awelde oure wyckenesse	*T'awelde* = to overcome
Wyth thy mercy	
And ful ous ay	*ful . . . ay* = fill us ever
Wyth thy nebshaftes blisse.	*thy nebshaftes blisse* = bliss of thy countenance
Thou boe nou oure ioie,	*boe nou* = are now
That shalt boen oure mede,	*mede* = reward

And oure woele ay boe in the   *ay boe = ever be*
That shalt ous wyth the nede.   *ous = us; nede = constrain*

Richard Rolle

One of the most powerful and influential religious voices in late medieval England belonged to the hermit, writer, and sometime chaplain Richard Rolle, born about 1290 (or 1300?) at Thornton Dale, near Pickering, in North Yorkshire. He attended, but did not graduate from, Oxford (and very doubtfully, the Sorbonne), but he lived, worked, and prayed as a hermit for more than 30 years, first close to his home, finally at Hampole, near Doncaster, where he may have acted as *de facto* chaplain to a convent of Cistercian nuns, who preserved his memory and wrote an account of his life intended to support his canonization, which, however, never transpired. His many works, in both Latin and English, were widely known not only in Britain but also in Europe, including the Rhineland, Sweden, and Switzerland, and particularly in Bohemia (there are many largely unstudied manuscripts of his works now preserved in Prague), where his writings were taken up by some of the late medieval reformers. Widely regarded, then as now, as a mystic, his English texts, particularly his spiritual guides, his meditations, and his lyrics, spoke to a clerical and (subsequently) a lay following, which was composed of both men and women, and which sought to encourage an affective, even an ecstatic, engagement of divine grace, and perhaps of a personally felt presence of the divine, as well. He lived much of his life as a well-known, often consulted hermit, dying in Hampole, conjecturally of the plague, in 1349.

See Hope Emily Allen, ed., *English Writings of Richard Rolle, Hermit of Hampole* (Oxford: Clarendon Press, 1931), which contains the works, edited from manuscript and printed here, and also Hope Allen's great work, *Writings Ascribed to Richard Rolle, Hermit of Hampole, and Materials for his Biography*, MLA Monograph Series, volume 3 (New York: D. C. Heath, and London: Oxford University Press, 1928, dated 1927). I have written the biography of this extraordinary scholar, one of the very first American women scholars to enjoy an international reputation, in: *Hope Emily Allen: Medieval Scholarship and Feminism* (Norman, Okla.: Pilgrim Books, 1988). The best introduction to Richard Rolle is now by Nicholas Watson, *Richard Rolle and the Invention of Authority*, Cambridge Studies in Medieval Literature 13 (Cambridge: Cambridge University Press, 1991).

B3

A Song of Love-longing to Jesus

IMEV 1715. Cambridge University Library MS Dd. 5. 64, part III, fols. 37–8. Brown B no. 83. Allen p. 41.

A powerful religious lyric; not without anti-semitism.

Ihesu, God sone, Lord of Mageste,
Send wil to my hert anly to couayte the. *anly = only*
Reue me lykyng of this land, my lufe that thou may be, *Reue = take away*
Take my hert intill thi hand, sett me in stabylte.

Ihesu, the mayden sone, that wyth thi blode me boght,
Thryl my sawule wyth thi spere, that mykel luf in men *Thryl = pierce;*
  hase wroght. *mykel = great*
Me langes, lede me to thi lyght, and festen in the al my *Me langes = I long*
  thoght.
In thi swetnes fyll my hert, my wa make wane till *wa = woe;*
  noght. *make wane = shrink*

Ihesu, my God, Ihesu my keyng, forsake noght my desyre.
My thoght make it to be meke, I hate bath pryde and ire.
Thi wil es my yhernyng, of lufe thou kyndel the fyre,
That I in swet lovyng with aungels take my hyre. *hyre = reward*

Wounde my hert within, and welde it at thi wille.
On blysse, that never sal blyn, thou gar me fest *blyn = cease; gar = make;*
  my skylle. *fest = fasten; skylle = reason*
That I thi lufe may wyn, of grace my thoght thou fylle,
And make me clene of syn, that I may come the tylle. *tylle = to*

Rote it in my hert, the memor of thi pyne, *Rote = fasten*
In sekenes and in qwert thi lufe be ever myne, *qwert = health*
My joy es al of the, my sawle, take it as thine.
My lufe ay waxand be, sa that it never dwyne. *ay = ever; dwyne = fade*

My sang es in syghyng, whil I dwel in this way. *sang = song, poem*
My lyfe es in langyng, that byndes me, nyght and day, *langyng = languishing*

Til I come til my kyng, that I won with hym may,   *til = to; won = dwell*
And se his fayre schynyng, and lyfe that lastes ay.

Langyng es in me lent, for lufe that I ne kan   *es . . . lent = has touched me;*
   lete.   *lete = forsake*
My lufe, it hase me schent, that ilk a bale may   *schent = hurt;*
   bete,   *ilk . . . bete = every evil amend*
Sen that my hert was brent in Cryste lufe sa swete,
Al wa fra me es went, and we sal never mete.

I sytt and syng of lufe-langyng, that in my hert es bred:
Ihesu, my kyng and my joyng, why ne war I to the led?   *war = was*
Ful wele I wate in al my state, in joy I sulde be fed.   *wate = know*
Ihesu, me bryng til thi wonyng, for blode that thou   *wonyng = dwelling*
   hase sched.

Demed he was to hyng, the faire aungels fode,
Ful sare thai gan hym swyng, when that he   *sare = sorrowfully;*
   bunden stode,   *swyng = beat; bunden = bound*
His bak was in betyng, and spylt hys blissed blode,
The thorn corond the keyng, that nayled was on the rode.   *corond = crowned*

Whyte was his naked breste, and rede his blody syde,
Wan was his faire face, his woundes depe and wyde.
The Iewyis wald not wande to pyne hym in   *Iewyis = Jews;*
   that tyde,   *wande = hesitate; tyde = time*
Als streme dose of the strande, his blode gan   *Als = as; strande = river*
   downe glyde.

Blynded was his faire ene, his flesch blody for bette,   *ene = eyes*
His lufsum lyf was layde ful low, and saryful   *vmbesette = encompassed*
   vmbesette.
Dede and lyf began to stryf whether mygth maystre mare,   *whether = which*
When aungels brede was dampned to dede, to safe oure   *sare = from*
   sauls sare.   *disease* (dative)

Lyf was slayne, and rase agayne, in fairehede may we fare,
And dede es broght til litel or noght, and kasten in endles kare.
On hym, that the boght, hafe al thi thoght, and lede the   *lare = teaching*
   in his lare.
Gyf al thi hert to Crist thi qwert, and lufe hym   *Gyf = give;*
   evermare.   *qwert = salvation*

B4

A Prose Lyric: Spiritual Joy in Jesus

Cambridge University Library MS Dd. 5. 64, fols. 41v–42, of the third division
of the manuscript, part III. Allen p. 51.

Allen notes, pp. 37–8, from a report on a contemporary manuscript gloss, that
Rolle wrote this "lyric" about 1343 when it had been prophesied to him on
Candlemas, the eve of the Purification of the Virgin (February 2), that he would
live for 12 more years, and that is why a presentiment of death runs through it.

Gastly gladnes [spiritual joy] in Ihesu, and ioy in hert, with swetnes in sawle
of the savor of heven in hope, es helth intil hele [health and salvation],
and my lyfe lendes [dwells] in luf, and lyghtsumnes [cheerfulness]
vnlappes [enfolds] my thoght. I drede noght, that me may wyrk wa [may
make me woeful], sa mykel I wate [know] of wele. It war na [no] wonder if dede war dere [dear (to me)], that I myght se hym that I seke. Bot
now it es lenthed [postponed] fra me, and me behoves lyf here, til he wil
me lese [release].

Lyst and lere of this lare [teaching], and the sal noght myslike. Lufe makes
me to melle, and joy gars me iangell [makes me speak]. Loke thow lede
thi lyf in lyghtsumnes, and hevynes, helde [keep] it away. Sarynes
[melancholy], lat it noght sytt wyth the, bot in gladnes of God evermare
make thow thi gle [joy]. Amen.

Embedded Lyrics of Richard Rolle

Rolle's embedded lyrics are not entirely different from Chaucer's, even though
they are inserted into a prose text, and Chaucer's are carefully integrated into a
continuing verse tale. In each case, however, they focus attention on a moment
or an idea of some importance and intensity, and encourage the reader to consider not only what is present in the surrounding text, but also in what its larger,
in this case religious, implications might be. But in Rolle as in Chaucer the lyrics
have a certain power which lets them stand alone, and offer a compelling
announcement of some at least of the mystic's continuing themes.

B5

Embedded Lyric A

Bodleian Library, Oxford MS Hatton 12 (*SC* 4127), fol. 85v. From *The English Psalter*, Psalm 56. Allen p. 15.

One of several short prayer-poems which appear with some regularity in several of Rolle's prose works. Though altogether appropriate to their place in the text, they also give the sense of a personal and felt outburst, and offer an opening onto the nature of the spirituality for which he was famous.

Ihesu, be thou my ioy,
Al melody and swetnes,
And lere me for to synge,   *lere = teach*
The sange of thi louynge.

B6

Embedded Lyric B

Cambridge University Library MS Ll.i.8, fol. 204. From *Meditations on the Passion*, Text I. Allen pp. 24–5.

A, Lord, kyng of myght, that levyn woldust thi   *levyn = leave, lay aside*
   myght,
And os unmyghty become, my wrongys to ryghte,   *os = as*
What is it that I speke and bete the wynd?
I speke of the felyng of the, and fynde I no taste,
I blondre in my wyrkyng, os man that is blynd.   *blondre = blunder*
I studye in my thoughtes, and thei wyrken al wast.   *wast = worse*
It is tokenyng of my deth and fylthe of my synne,
That slayn hath my sowle, and stoke is thereynne,
And stoppyth al the sauoure that I may nought the fele,
That so schamely haue ben thi tretoure untrewe.   *tretoure = traitor*

B7

Embedded Lyric C

Bodleian Library, Oxford MS e Museo 232 (*SC* 3657), fol. 3v. From *Meditations on the Passion*, Text II. Allen p. 30.

To loue the,
Swete Ihesu,
Is most medeful,   *medeful = rewarding*
Most spedeful   *spedeful = effectual*
And most nedefulle.

John Audelay

John Audelay had not the proto-celebrity of Richard Rolle or the academic standing of William Herebert, and his works, 55 poems, are preserved in a single manuscript, MS Douce 302 (*Summary Catalogue* 21876), now in the Bodleian Library, Oxford. Audelay's birth and death dates are unknown, but a colophon dated 1426 in Douce 302 attests that the author was a chaplain (*capellanus*), and that he was both deaf and blind (*secus et surdus*); he also attests to his own blindness. He is further identified with both Haghmond Abbey near Shrewsbury, and with one Lord Strange, whom his editor has identified with Richard le Strange, who held the title "Lord Strange of Knokin" from 1397–1449.

His *oeuvre* has been published by Ella Keats Whiting, ed., *The Poems of John Audelay*, EETS OS 184 (London: Early English Text Society, 1931), and there is a good recent introduction by Eric Stanley, "The Verse Forms of Jon the Blynde Awdelay," in Helen Cooper and Sally Mapstone, eds., *The Long Fifteenth Century: Essays for Douglas Gray* (Oxford: Clarendon Press, 1997), pp. 99–121.

B8

Of the Love of God

IMEV 831. Bodleian Library MS Douce 302, fol. 30v. Greene no. 272. Whiting no. 50.

Audelay's gentle reflection, in a carol, upon what he and many of his contemporaries would have regarded as the greatest of medieval themes, the love which exists between God and all of humankind.

I haue a loue is heuen kyng,
I loue his loue fore euermore.

Fore loue is loue and euer schal be,
And loue has bene ore we were bore.   ore = ere, before
Fore loue he askys no nother fe,   nother = other; fe = fee, reward
Bot loue agayn, he kepys no more,   kepys = wants
I say herefore.

I haue a loue . . .

Trew loue is tresoure, trust is store,
To a loue to Godis plesyng.
Bot leued loue makis men e-lore,   leued = ignorant; e-lore = lost
To loue here lust and here lykyng,   lust = desire; lykyng = pleasure
I say herefore.

I haue a loue . . .

In good loue ther is no syn,
Without loue is heuenes,
Herefore to loue I nyl not blyn,   nyl = will not; blyn = cease
To loue my God and his goodnes,
I say herefore.

I haue a loue . . .

For he me louyd or I hym knew,
Therfore I loue him alther best,   alther best = best of all

Ellis my loue I myght hit rew.
I loue with him to take my rest,
I say herefore.

I haue a loue . . .

Of al loueres that euer was borne,
His loue hit passid euerechon.   euerechon = *every one*
Nad he vs louyd, we were forelorne,   *Nad He* = *had he not; forelorne* = *lost*
With[out h]is loue, trew loue is non,   *[. . .]* = MS omission
I say herefore.

I haue a loue . . .

B9

Of Our King, Henry VI

IMEV 822. Bodleian Library MS Douce 302, fols. 29–29v. Greene no. 428. Whiting no. 39.

This is a somewhat conflicted carol – insofar as that word can reasonably be applied to Audelay's poetry. It concerns the personal resolve and military prowess of King Henry V (1386–1422, reigned 1413–22) as much as the putative saintliness of King Henry VI (1421–71, reigned 1422–61 and 1470–1), whose reputation for holiness was celebrated in contemporary and later lyrics, but whose reign, part of which was spent in a coma, cannot be judged a success in terms either political or military – though the king's own interests were elsewhere, and he did found both Eton College and King's College, Cambridge, in the course of it.

In connection with another poem in praise of Henry VI, Douglas Gray points out that the king's Carthusian chaplain reported that Henry dressed simply, and often wore a hair-shirt under his robes (Gray no. 69). There is a manuscript in the Bodleian Library, MS Don. e. 120, known as the Pudsay Hours, which seems to have had an association with the king. A family tradition noted by James Raine held that after the Battle of Hexham King Henry took refuge with the Pudsay family at Balton Hall, and the manuscript contains a Latin prayer addressed to King Henry, a Latin poem in his honor, and also a Middle English lyric (*Supplement* 333.5) which testifies even more directly to the veneration in which this putatively saintly king was held:

As far as hope will [ ] yn length	[ ] = word missing
On the, Kyng Henry, I fix my mynde.	
That be my prayour: I may have strenkith	*my* = MS *thy*
In vertuous lyfe my warkes to bynde.	*bynde* = *hold fast*
Though I to the haue ben vnkynde,	
Off wilfulnesse long tyme and space,	
Off forgeuenesse I ask the grace.	
Hop hathe me meuyde to seke	*Hop* = *hope*; *meuyde* = *moved, prompted*
this place,	
In trust off socore by thyn olde properte.	
Was neuer man cam beforene thi face,	
Rebellion or oder yn aduersite,	*oder yn* = *in other*
Off thyn compassion commaundid them goo free.	
Now, for thi pety to Hym that all schall deme,	*pety* = *pity*
Pray for me thy seruaunt and pilgreme. (fol. 4).	

Audelay's spirited carol assumes the conventional piety present in the Pudsay lyric too, but seeks to add to it a new national sentiment, which can be identified in other fifteenth-century poems (see for example no. 49, above). Thus in Audelay's poem King Henry V's victory at Agincourt is as highly praised as his son's less martial accomplishments, and the narrative resolves itself into a poem celebrating both English piety and English kingship, in the course of which Henry VI emerges as not only admirable in his own right, but also as the recipient of the benefits, both personal and national, associated with his father's military success. There are other contemporary and near-contemporary tributes to Henry VI's piety in *IMEV* 936, 2218, 2445, and 2393. See too John Watts, *Henry VI and the Politics of Kingship* (Cambridge: Cambridge University Press, 1997); Paul Grosjean, SJ, *Henrici VI Angliae Regis: miracula postuma ex codice Musei Britannici Regio 13. C. VIII*, Subsidia Hagiographica 22 (Brussels: Soc. Bollandistes, 1935), and James Raine, "The Pudsays of Barford," *Archaeologia Aeliana*, Society of Antiquaries of Newcastle-upon-Tyne, NS 2 (1858): 173–90.

A! Perles Pryns to the we pray,
Saue our kyng both nyght and day!

Fore he is ful yong, tender of age,
Semele to se, o bold corage,   *Semele = attractive; o = of*
Louele and lofte of his lenage,   *lofte = high*
Both perles prince and kyng veray.   *veray = truly*

A! Perles Pryns . . .

His gracious granseres and his grawndame,   *granseres = grandsires*
His fader and moderis of kyngis thay came;
Was neuer a worthear prynce of name,
So exelent in al our day.

A! Perles Pryns . . .

His fader, fore loue of mayd Kateryn,   *His fader = i.e., King Henry V*
In Fraunce he wroght turment and tene.   *tene = prospered*
His loue hee sayd hit schuld not   trans. = *he (the Dauphin) forbad*
   ben   *his (Henry V's) love of Katherine*
And send him ballis him with to play.   *ballis = tennis balls*

A! Perles Pryns . . .

Then was he wyse in wars with alle,
And taght Franchemen to plai at the balle,
With tenes hold he ferd ham   trans. = *with tennis of old he frightened them all*
   halle,
To castelles and setis thai floyn away.   *setis = seats; floyn = fled*

A! Perles Pryns . . .

To Harflete a sege he layd anon,
And cast a bal vnto the towne,
The Frenchemen swere be se and sun,   *se = sea*
Hit was the fynd that mad that fray.

A! Perles Pryns . . .

Anon thai toke ham to cownsele,
Oure gracious kyng thai wold asayle,
At Agyncowrt at that batayle,
The floure of Frawnce he fel that day.   *fel = struck down*

A! Perles Pryns . . .

The kyng of Frawns then was agast,
Mesagers to him send in hast,
Fore wele he west hit was bot wast   *west = knew; wast = a waste*
Hem to witstond in hone way.   *in hone way = in any way*

A! Perles Pryns . . .

And prayd hym to sese of his outrage,
And take Kateryn to mareage.
Al Frawnce to hym schuld do homage,
And croune him kyng afftyr his day.

A! Perles Pryns . . .

Of Frawnce he mad him anon regent,
And wedid Kateren in his present.
Into Englond anon he went,   *anon = at once*
And cround our quene in ryal aray.

A! Perles Pryns . . .

Of quen Kateryn our kyng was borne,
To saue our ryght that was forelorne,   *forelorne = lost*
Oure faders in Frawns had won beforne,
Thai han hit hold mone a day.   *mone = many*

A! Perles Pryns . . .

Thus was his fader a conqueroure,
And wan his moder with gret onoure.   *onoure = honor*
Now may the kyng bere the floure
Of kyngis and kyngdams in vche cuntre.   *vche = each*

A! Perles Pryns . . .

Of him schal fal the prophece,   *fal = befall*
That hath ben sayd of Kyng Herre,
The hole cros wyn or he dye,   *hole = holy; or = ere, before*
That Crist halud on Good Fryday.   *halud = hallowed*

A! Perles Pryns . . .

Al wo and werres he schal a-cese,
And set alle reams in rest and pese,
And turne to Cristyndam al hethynes,
Now grawnt him hit so be may.

A! Perles Pryns . . .

Pray we that Lord is Lord of alle,
To saue our kyng, his reme ryal,   *reme ryal = royal realm*
And let neuer myschip vppon him fall,
Ne false traytoure him to betray.

A! Perles Pryns . . .

I pray youe, Seris, of your gentre,
Syng this carol reuerently,
Fore it is mad of Kyng Herre,
Gret ned fore him we han to pray.   *ned = need*

A! Perles Pryns . . .

Yif he fare wele, wele schul we be,
Or ellis we may be ful sore,
Fore him schal wepe mone an e,   *mone an e = many an eye*
Thus prophecis the blynd Awdlay.

A! Perles Pryns . . .

Appendix C: Three Poems from the Findern Anthology

The three poems which follow, together with no. 18 above, appear in the Findern Anthology, a fifteenth-century paper manuscript containing an anthology of secular poetry together with a few other indications, including a medieval butcher's bill, which together suggest that the manuscript was treated by its first owners as an object of everyday use. It is now preserved in Cambridge University Library, MS Ff.1.6. Part of its interest stems from the fact that some of the scribes who wrote the manuscript and also some of the authors of the lyrics were undoubtedly women, and the manuscript as a whole makes up one of the earliest collections of women's poetry preserved in English.

The manuscript was first brought to critical attention by Rossell Hope Robins in "The Findern Anthology," *PMLA* 69 (1954): 610–42, but its association with women emerges in two later studies, Elizabeth Hanson-Smith, "A Woman's View of Courtly Love: The Findern Anthology, Cambridge University Library MS Ff.1.6," *Journal of Women's Studies in Literature* 1 (1979): 179–94, and especially Sarah McNamer, "Female Authors, Provincial Setting: The Reversing of Courtly Love in the Findern Manuscript," *Viator* 22 (1991): 279–310. McNamer's seminal study demonstrated women's authorship for 15 of the lyrics which she printed (her no. 8 appears as no. 18, above, her other numbers are listed under her name below), and argued for the presence of a new genre of Middle English lyric poetry, that of the non-paradic woman's lament, which involved both courtly and literary idiom, and felt human experience. In formulating her category she identified the clear, distinct, and self-expressive voice of fifteenth-century Englishwomen living in the provinces.

There is a facsimile edition of this fascinating manuscript edited by Richard Beadle and A. E. B. Owen, *The Findern Anthology, Cambridge University Library MS Ff.1.6* (London: Scolar Press, 1977). It has been studied in detail by Kate

Harris, "The Origins and Make-up of Cambridge University Library MS Ff.1.6," *Transactions of the Cambridge Bibliography Society* 8 (1983): 299–333, and by Ralph Hanna, "The Production of Cambridge University Library MS Ff.1.6," *Studies in Bibliography* 40 (1987): 62–70.

C1

IMEV 4059, fol. 20v. McNamer no. 1.

A moving, even powerful poem, in which a woman attests to her love of her husband. It easily, almost offhandedly, brushes aside the usual anti-feminist stereotypes in favor of a felt statement of marital love and affection.

Where Y haue chosyn, stedefast woll Y be,
Newyre to repente in wyll, thowt ne dede,   *Newyre = never*
Yow to sarue watt ye commaund me,   *watt = what*
Neuer hyt withdrawe for no maner drede.
Thus am Y bownd by yowre godelyhede,
Wych hathe me causyd, and that in euery wyse
Wyle I in lyfe endure, to do yow my servyse.

Yowre desertt can none odere deserue,   *desertt = deserving; odere = other*
Wych ys in my remembrauns both day and nyght.
Afore al creaturus I yow loue and serue
Wyle in thys world I haue strength and myght,
Wych ys in dewte, of very dwe ryght,
By promys made with feythful assuraunce,
Euer to yow sarue withowtyn varyaunce.   *varyaunce = changing, unfaithfulness*

C2

IMEV 3917, fol. 56. Davies no. 134. Duncan B no. 39. McNamer no. 4.

This poem concerns itself with the game of Love, but does so with an amused
sophistication which almost entirely hides a tone of warning which lies just below
the surface. Its narrative setting is conventional, but it is a studied convention-
ality which lays spring-guns and man-traps as it goes.

Whatso men seyn
Loue is no peyn
To them, serteyn,
Butt varians.

peyn = pain
serteyn = certain
varians = variation, treachery

For they constreyn
Ther hertis to feyn,
Ther mowthis to pleyn
Ther displesauns.

feyn = pretend
pleyn = complain

Whych is indede
Butt feyned drede,
So God me spede,
And dowbilnys.

feyned = pretended
dowbilnys = duplicity

Ther othis to bede,
Ther lyuys to lede,
And profer mede –
Newfangellnys!

bede = tell
profer = MS proferith; mede = reward
trans. = is only fashionable novelty

For when they pray,
Ye shall haue nay,
Whatso they sey,
Beware – for shame!

nay = nothing

For euery daye
They waite ther pray
Wherso they may,
And make but game.

pray = prey

Then semyth me
Ye may well se

They be so fre
In euery plase.

Hitt were pete

pete = pity

Butt they shold be
Begelid, parde,

Begelid = beguiled, fooled

Withowtyn grace.

C3

IMEV 657, fol. 138v–139. Davies no. 137. McNamer no. 9.

This poem plays with the connection between Fortune and memory, while taking seriously the conventions of secular love poetry, and at the same time recording a felt response to a lover's absence.

Continvaunce   *Continvaunce = continuation*
Of remembraunce
Withowte endyng
Doth me penaunce,
And gret greuaunce
For yowr partyng.   *For = because of*

So depe ye be
Grauen, parde,   *Grauen = engraved*
Withyn myn hert
That afore mee
Euer I yow see
In thought couert.   *couert = hidden*

Though I ne playn   *ne playn = do not complain (against)*
My wofull payn
But bere yt styll,
It were in vayn
To sey agayn
Fortunes wyll.

Glossary

Many of the words identified in the side glosses to the poems are omitted; "y" is sometimes treated as "i;" and the Middle English forms listed are those which appear in the edition.

a (prep.)   at, on, in, from
adoun   down
afore   before
ak   but
almest   hardly, almost
als   as, also
also   also, as, so
ame   am
and, ant   and, if
anon   at once
appele   accuse, appeal against
appil   apple
ar(n)   are
aray   display, splendor, dress
arest(e)   rests, stops
armys   arms, coat-of-arms
asterte   escape, get away
atte   at
atyre   dress, attire
avayll   help, assistance
awayward   away (from), aside
axe (v.)   ask, demand
aye   ever
ayens(t)   against

babyr   protruding, baboon-like
baldely   boldly, forcefully
balys   sufferings, baleful events
bar (v.)   bore, carried
batayle   battle
bath   both
baundoun   power, thrall, control
bedde (n.)   bed
bely   belly, stomach
bemene   pity
berst the pris   have preeminence
beshrewyd   cursed
beste (n.)   beast
besynesse   occupation, being busy, activity
bett   beaten, thrashed
betuene   between
bewte   beauty
byde   wait, await
biheve   behooves, is necessary for
bileeue   faith, religious belief
bigint   begins
byll   letter, missive
bisek   beseech, entreat

blent blinds
blys bliss (especially of heaven)
blithe happy, joyous
blody bloody
blow(e) brag, boast; blow
bok(es) book(s)
bolstar pillow (especially for a bed)
bon (n.) bone
bone petition
bos is necessary
boste boast, brag
bot but
bote (n.) remedy, salvation
bounte generosity, bounty
bour bedroom, inner chamber
bowge bottle, carrier
bulluc bullock
but but, unless, except for
but if unless

catte cat
cause reason, because of
che she
che(e)re appearance, joy, mood, demeanor
chelde cold, chill
clere clear, shine brightly
clymbyng ambition
cok cock (both senses)
comly attractive, comely
cors body, corpse
coste cost, coast
countre country
couth could, knew how
cum come
cuntre country

dayis (gen.) day's
dele be intimate with; deal with; divide
demaeyne demesne, possession

dere dear, beloved
derusion scorn, derision
deuyne divine, understand
dey die
dysdayene disdain, despise
dissaite deceit, deception
doe (v.) do, give
dolour sorrow, pain (especially psychological)
dowe, dowve dove
dowtles certainly, without doubt
dublett doublet, padded outer jacket
dure endure, sustain

e eye
ech each
eche eternal
ej alas!
eke also
eldyth grows old, ages
ele hell
ellis otherwise, else
encrece increase
endyte write, inscribe
enrote establish, fix
ere ear
ert are
es is
estaat estate, social class
esye easy
euerech(e) every
ey egg
eyen, eynen, ene eyes

fadir, fader(s) father, fathers
fayn welcome, glad
faynyng pretending, feigning
fal fall, befall
fallyt falls
fals false, misleading

fand found, discovered
fareth goes, fares
fauoryd favored
fawcon falcon
fel left me; struck down, slew
felde field
fest fasten, fix
fete feet
feture(ys) feature(s)
feye fated, doomed
fikel fickle, changeable
fisses (pl.) fish
forelorne lost, destitute
for soth(e) in truth
foules birds, fowls
flatte flat
flod water, sea
flore floor
flytte fled
fo foe, enemy
fontane fountain
forwake exhausted, tired out
foryefnes forgiveness, pardon,
  absolution
fote foot
foweles fowls, birds
fowre four
fra from
fre gracious, generous
frith woods, wooded lands
fro, frome from
ful very

galauntyne a jellied sauce
  especially for fish
gar(s) make(s)
garmentes clothes, garments
gent, gentyl, genitil noble, enobled
get, geitt black, jet
geth goes
gewrt works to bring about, causes

glose gloss, explanation
go good
god (adj.) good
godely goodly
gorel pig
gostly spiritual, holy
goth(e) goes
grad cried out, announced
granseres grandfathers
grawndame grandmother
grene green
grest greatest
gret(e) great, noble; nobility

haf have
hald hold
halud hallowed, made holy
hammys hams (of a leg)
hede notice, warning
helpit helps it
hem them
hendy lucky, clever
henne hence, far away
heore their
herbere orchard, garden
here rabbit, hare
hert(e) heart; male deer
hew(e) color, complexion,
  appearance
hewid head
hext highest
hit, hyt it
ho who
hod hood
hokyd hamstrung, made lame
hold, holt hold, held
hol(e) (adj.) whole; holy
ho(o)le (n.) hole
holly wholly
hondin hands
hone delay, hold back

hors horse
hou(h) how
hur, hyr her
hyng(e) hung, hang

iantilnesse nobility, gentility
Ic, Ich I
ilast lasts, endures
ilk same, the same
intil into, to
iocound joyful, happy
iprikit stuck, pricked
istickit pierced

kuyndes natures
kynd(e) nature

ladde led
langyng love-longing
lare lore, teaching
lat(e), laten (v.) let
le(e)ueth believe
le(e)ve leave
lef dear, precious
lem(m)an lover (sometimes with the connotation of illicit)
lenage lineage
leorneth learns
ler(n)e learn, teach
leve leave off, abandon
lhude loud
lych like, alike
lyghtsumnes joy, cheerfulness
lyht light(/s)
lytyl, litel little, small, tiny
lofe love
lofte high, above
loke look, see
lomb lamb
lossom lovely, loveable
loth loathsome, hateful

loue-longing(e) the expectation or experience of love, love-longing
lufe love
luffed loved, beloved
lufsum lovely, beloved
lustnes pleases, pleasure
lutel little
lysse restores peace and joy; solaces
lyst rest, remain, lie

ma(a)d made
may, mayde maiden, virgin
maistrey mastery
mak(e) (n.) mate, lover
makeles without peer, without a mate or lover, without stain (especially a spiritual stain, without sin)
makis (v.) makes
manly like a man, with courage
med(e) meed, reward; meadow
mekyl, michel, mulch much, great
mete food
meue move to talk about, discuss
mirie merry, happy
mysgrowen misshapen, twisted
mo(o) more
mo(o)der, mo(o)dir mother
mon man, person; must
mone moon; many
mony many
mor moor, a desolate expanse of unproductive and wild land
mort dead
mot must
mow(e)(n) may, be able
mownt, mownteyn mountain, hill
mutable changing, mutable

narre near
narw close, narrow
nat not
ne nor
nede want, poverty, need
ner(e) near
nye close
nis, nys is not
nist night
noght not
non any, none
notus notes (of music)
nout not
n(o)u now
nu new, now
nuwe new

o one
oder, odyr other
off of
on on, one
ony any
onys once
onoure honor
opynd opened, exposed
or ere, before
os as, us
other other, and
oule owl
ous us
owght anything; aught (to)
owt out

payne(ys) pain(s)
paleis palace
pall shrouds
pappe teat, nipple
parde by God, certainly
pase (v.) pass
pease, peis, peys peace

pere peer, equal
perles peerless
pyk pike (the fish)
pine regret, suffering
piteuouse pitiable, piteous
pitt(e), put pit, grave, hell
pre(e)s crowd, the many
present presence
preve prove, test
primerole primrose, a wild red rose
  of uncertain symbolic significance
pris(e), prys worth, excellence,
  praise

quene, qwen queen
qwert salvation

raue rave, become mad
refut refuge, retreat
renne run
reuerense reverence, adore, love
reuful pitiful, sad
reve tear away from, take from
reynes rains
ryal royal
ryght very
rynd thorny bark
rynne run
rywe rue
ro(o)d(e) (n.) cross, face
roshen rush
roun words, speech, poem

saferon saffron, red-orange (a
  blush?)
saynte saint, holy
sal shall
sang song
satyne satin
savor taste, savor

sawle soul
sche she
schent terrified, destroyed
sclep sleep
se (n.) sea, ocean
seche seek, search
sed (n.) seed
sege seige, assault
semeliour more attractive, more beautiful
semlokest most attractive
sen (adv.) since
se(e)(n) (v.) see, look at, understand
sentence meaning, significance
serue serve
sese cease
sey tell, say
shad shed
shuld(e) should
sister sister, cousin, lover
syth, seth since
skorne scorn, have contempt for
slep sleep
small(e) small, thin, soft
smert pain, hurt
snelle active, quick
snough snow
socour help, succor
son(n)e (n.) son, sun
sonnes (gen.) sun's
soth truth
sothfastnesse truth, certainty
sport entertainment, play
spray a branch (in bloom)
sterre star
stilly silent
stokkes stocks
stunte stop
suehte sweet one

suetyth entreating
suffise be content with, hold sufficient
sum some
swilk such
swink labor, toil
swyre neck, throat
swon swan

tayle tail
tapers tapers, candles
te (prep.) to, toward
te (def. art.) the
thaugh although
the (pron.) thee, you (sing.)
tho those, these; then
tholien suffer, endure
thorw(out) through(out)
thow(e) thou, you (sing.)
thowt thought
thrall slave, thrall
thryfte profit, success
tyde time, hour, occasion
tydyng event, news
til, tyl, tylle until, to
to (n.) toe
tofore before
toke took
tonne barrel, tun
trace study, examine
tre tree, wood, cross
treu, trew true
treu lofe truelove
trippede tripped
tuycion protection
turuf turf, grass placed over a grave
tuur tower
twyne (v.) part
twynkelyng twinkling, winking of eye

ut out

vaile valley (especially of the world)
variant changeable
varyaunce alteration
vche, vchon(e) each
velanye villainy, wrong-doing
verray true
vysage face, visage
vncurts discourteous, rude
vndir under, lower
vppon upon
vpsedon upside down
vre our
vs us

wa woe
waite await
wak wake
wald would
walwed smothered (as with a sauce)
wan pale, white; when; won
wande hesitate
war was
wast worse
wat what
wauyng waving
wedyr weather
wele wealth, well-being
wen when
wene (v.) think, expect, know
wep weep
wepinde weeping
weren were
werres wars, battles
west knew
wham whom
wher where, whether
whye why
whon when

wyf wife, woman
wyn wine
winnen win
wynter winter(s), years
wisdam wisdom, understanding
wyse way, manner
wyst knew
wit(h) with
witen know
witte, wyte (n.) wit, mind, understanding
witterly truly, with knowledge
wnne delight, pleasure
wo woe
wod (n.) wood, forest, cross; (adj.) mad
won wan, pale
wonder (v.) marvel, wonder
wondyr(ed) (adv.) marvellously, strangely, wonderfully
wonyng dwelling, abode
wore pool
woreld world
worilde world
wos whose
wose whoever
wot know(s)
wowe woo, court
wowndes wounds
wowndyd wounded
wroght made, created
wy why
wyght creature, person
wyse manner, way
wyter knowing, wise

ych each
yede went, drew near
yef, yf(f) if, that
yftis gifts, presents
yhent seized, grasped, got

yn(n) in
Ynglysch English
yong young
yow you

ys is
yt it
ywys indeed, certainly
yynge young

A Short Bibliography of the Middle English Lyric

The books relevant to the lyric listed in this bibliography should help students find useful assistance in studying or writing about the lyrics printed here. The following three resources are helpful in surveying certain aspects of both the medieval lyric and the Middle English lyric.

1 *A Concordance to the Middle English Shorter Poem* by Michael J. Preston, 2 volumes, Compendia: Computer-Generated Aids to Literary and Linguistic Research, volume 6 (Leeds: W. S. Maney and Son, 1975).

2 An excellent annotated bibliography by Rosemary Greentree, *The Middle English Lyric and Short Poem*, Annotated Bibliographies of Old and Middle English Literature, volume VII (Cambridge: D. S. Brewer, 2001), which contains references to studies carried out both on the Middle English lyric as a whole, and on individual lyrics. References to ballad literature and to carols appear in parts IX and X of this anthology.

3 Though more remains to be done in this field, the music which animated Middle English and other medieval lyrics has been studied and recorded in an excellent project entitled *The Medieval Lyric*, directed by Margaret Switten, and supported jointly by the National Endowment for the Humanities and Mount Holyoke College (1988–2001), which has published in Anthology III, CD 5, a recorded selection of medieval English lyrics, and *Medieval English Lyric*, an accompanying anthology and commentary by Howell D. Chickering, Jr. (South Hadley, Mass.: Mount Holyoke College, 1989). The web site is: http://www.mtholyoke.edu/acad/medst/medieval lyric/staff.html.

Critical Studies

Karin Boklund-Lagopoulou, *'I have a yong suster': Popular Song and the Middle English Lyric* (Dublin: Four Courts Press, 2002). A considered treatment not only of the influence of popular song on the Middle English lyric, but also of the importance of manuscripts in their preservation, and of critical theory, too. It treats as well, and in a traditionally historical context, ballads and carols, imagination and enchantment, heroism and gender, together with the codes which variously inform the implied world of the poems.

Peter Dronke, *The Medieval Lyric*, third edition (Cambridge: D. S. Brewer, 1996). There was a New York edition of the first London edition (1968) published in The Perennial Library of Harper & Row in 1969. Dronke's pioneering work focused upon the medieval poet's originality and innovation, which was not the usual approach at the time. It influenced early studies, comparative and critical, of the Middle English lyric, by generating interest in medieval poetic originality and in the medieval Latin lyric itself, which was (and to a degree remains) understudied. His *Medieval Latin and the Rise of European Love-Lyric*, second edition, 2 volumes (Oxford: Clarendon Press, 1968), remains the major book in the field of medieval Latin lyric. *The Medieval Lyric* contains criticism of Middle English lyrics, and its text has remained constant over three editions; though useful bibliographical entries have been added, relatively few of these concern English lyrics. A student may read with confidence whichever edition is available of this excellent and wide-ranging introduction to the medieval lyric.

Douglas Gray, *Themes and Images in the Medieval English Religious Lyric* (London and Boston: Routledge & Kegan Paul, 1972). The best critical reading of the Middle English religious lyric, Gray, who published the collection of Middle English religious lyrics listed in the Abbreviations and cited at the head of many of the lyrics in this edition, develops both close readings of individual religious lyrics, and an exposition of their intellectual and cultural background. Its great strength lies in the way it reveals the cultural and poetic traditions out of which the poets worked, while remaining particularly sensitive to their departure from those traditions, a departure which led to their originality and innovation.

Anne L. Klinck and Ann Marie Rasmussen, eds., *Medieval Woman's Song: A Cross-Cultural Approach*, The Middle Ages Series (Philadelphia: University of Pennsylvania Press, 2002). With particular attention to women's voice, this anthology surveys the range of medieval European writing by women, and contains an excellent treatment of the Middle English tradition by Judith M. Bennett, "Ventriloquisms: When Maidens Speak in English Songs," pp. 187–204.

Stephen Manning, *Wisdom and Number: Toward a Critical Appraisal of the Middle English Religious Lyric* (Lincoln: University of Nebraska Press, 1962). One of the earlier studies of the Middle English religious lyric, Manning sometimes seems to be apologizing for the poems he is writing about, though many of his individual readings are considered, perceptive, and good.

Arthur K. Moore, *The Secular Lyric in Middle English* (Lexington: University of Kentucky Press, 1951). An early and engaged account of the Middle English secular lyric based on articles Moore published between 1948 and 1951. The organization of these lyrics which Moore proposed has not been widely accepted, but readings of individual lyrics retain interest.

Raymond Oliver, *Poems Without Names: The English Lyric, 1200–1500* (Berkeley, Los Angeles, London: University of California Press, 1970). An analytical, rather than a critical reading of many now-familiar lyrics, this study is not long on historical examination, though its metrical analysis is often useful.

Edmund Reiss, *The Art of the Middle English Lyric: Essays in Criticism* (Athens, Ga.: University of Georgia Press, 1972). In spite of the subtitle this study is touched, though not controlled, by exegetical criticism popular at the time, but is sensitive to language and diction, often constructed theologically.

Sarah Appleton Weber, *Theology and Poetry in the Middle English Lyric: A Study of Sacred History and Aesthetic Form* (Columbus, Ohio: Ohio State University Press, 1969). A considered reading of the theological dimension of the Middle English religious lyric, particularly as it relates to time, written at a time when such studies were in short supply and the religious aspects of the poems often required apology. It is concerned above all with the poems' religious background, and is most useful with poems where the author's own aesthetic fits convincingly.

Siegfried Wenzel, *Preachers, Poets and the Early English Lyric* (Princeton: Princeton University Press, 1986). A specialized, perceptive, and learned study which documents the association of the lyric with preaching, a relationship which had not been widely understood before Wenzel wrote. The study is also concerned with the hymn tradition, and above all with the influence of the sermon.

Rosemary Woolf, *The English Religious Lyric in the Middle Ages* (Oxford: Clarendon Press, 1968). A monumental work, pioneering in its day and still of great importance. Perhaps best for its understanding of the development and movement of the Middle English lyric as a whole, though also attentive to the interpretation and the aesthetic of particular lyrics. Woolf examines individual poems revealingly, often by setting them within rather than against a literary tradition with which she has herself identified.

First Line Index

I have listed the first lines of the lyrics printed here, and in order to help speed the identification of a partly remembered song, where there is a burden (a refrain) I have listed the first line of that as well. Where the number is preceded by A, B, or C the entry refers to the relevant appendix; where it is followed by a letter, it refers to a specific version of the poem in question.

Manuscript Index

Because I have made the 1982 edition *The Minor Poems of Geoffrey Chaucer*, The Variorum Edition, volume V part one, published by the University of Oklahoma Press and edited by George B. Pace and Alfred David, the base text from which I have edited the poems recorded in Appendix A, I have not listed the Chaucer manuscripts listed there. Chaucer's embedded lyrics, as noted, I have edited from the facsimile of the Hengwrt Manuscript edited by Paul G. Ruggiers (1979). A letter followed by a number indicates the poem's number within an appendix; a number followed by a letter indicates a version within a number.

Cambridge

University Library
MS Dd.5.64, Part III, fol. 37 (no. B3),
   fol. 41v (no. B4)
MS Ff.1.6, fol. 20v (no. C1), fol. 56
   (no. C2), fol. 137v (no. 18), fol. 138v
   (no. C3)
MS Hh.4.12, fol. 44v (no. 17)
MS Ii.III.8, fol. 111 (no. 30)
MS Ll.i.8, fol. 204 (no. B6)

Gonville and Caius College
MS 383, p. 41 (no. 40)

Trinity College

MS 323, fol. 24v (no. 14), fol. 47v (no. 5),
   fol. 83v (no. 27)
MS 1157, fol. 69 (no. 28)

London

British Library
Additional MS 31922, fol. 37v (no. 50)
Additional MS 46919, fol. 207v (no. B1),
   209v (no. B2)
Arundel MS 285, fol. 196v (no. 15)
Arundel MS 292, fol. 3v (no. 4)
Egerton MS 613, fol. 2 (no. 14)
Harley MS 541, fol. 207v (no. 12C)
Harley MS 682, fol. 88v (no. 10)
Harley MS 978, fol. 11v (no. 8)
Harley MS 2253, fol. 63v (no. 31)
Royal MS 17 D vi, fol. 3 (no. 34)
Royal MS Appendix 58, fol. 5 (no. 37)
Sloane MS 1584, fol. 45v (no. 48)
Sloane MS 2593, fol. 10v (no. 13 and
   no. 39), fol. 11 (no. 9 and no. 33),
   fol. 32 (no. 16)
Sloane MS 3534, fol. 3v (no. 12A)